"Christian Coon has experienced the radical transformation that resurrection life can offer, in his life and in his ministry. He will take you from failure to thriving, from death to life, as you witness the power of the Holy Spirit, leading him through struggle into vital ministry and vital living."

—Martin Lee, Director of Congregational Development
and Redevelopment, Northern Illinois Conference,
The United Methodist Church

Failing Boldly is an important word for all faithful followers of Jesus. Christian reminds us that when we attempt great things for God, everything won't always go as we pray and expect. By honestly relating his personal journey, he gives us hope and courage to get back up and keep moving forward."

—Mike Crawford, Coordinator for Congregational
Development, Illinois Great Rivers Conference,
The United Methodist Church

"Christian Coon's clear, open, and conversational writing style is as if we are sitting down to share a beer, a meal, a walk, or a coffee. He has much to say here. He and Trey Hall have connected so many dots in unique and creative ways as they participate in culture, wrestle with the times, and integrate the biblical and theological traditions and UMC heritage. What makes it all so powerful and accessible for me is Coon leads with his vulnerability, honesty, story, and experience. I was immediately led to my own story and experiences and found myself able to remember, own, and connect my learning or need to learn with his shared wisdom and experience."

—Ray Schulte, Managing Director,
The Center for Parish Development

"With just the right amount of humor, humility, and honesty, Christian Coon boldly invites us into his personal life, and allows us to accompany him on the journey–the good and the bad—of planting Urban Village. There is holy irony in successfully writing a book on failure, and he captures it with sensitivity and grace by sharing his heartfelt experiences and introducing us to other writers, both historical and contemporary, unpacking failure through the prism of spirituality. *Failing Boldly* is a practical book that points to many ways to look at and learn from failing; but mainly it points to Jesus."

—Jim Ozier, Director of New Church Development and
Congregational Transformation, North Texas Conference,
The United Methodist Church

"With *Failing Boldly*, Christian Coon provides a much-needed antidote to the success-driven "Hero Pastor" library of church leadership books. His honest and courageous self-reflection on the ups and downs of ministry make this a must-read for church leaders of all kinds. Learning to embrace and learn from failure, even though it hurts, is the path toward reclaiming joy and fun in the midst of the anxious and overly earnest church in America. I greatly enjoyed this book, and I will be recommending it to the pastors and church planters whom I teach and coach."

—Curtis Brown, New Church Strategist,
Path 1 Discipleship Ministries,
The United Methodist Church

"Failing Boldly gives me great hope and excitement for the future of the church. The story of Urban Village continues to unfold and inspire. Christian Coon shares the good, the bad, and the ugly in this engaging, no-holds-barred resource. The reader will actually walk away from this with honest, practical, and realistic wisdom to better understand the call, how to create a unique new worshiping community, and how to succeed by failing. Even through the scars, Coon articulates why the reward are worth the risk. Want to impact your community? Read this book."

—Brad Aycock, Director of New Church Development,
West Ohio Conference, The United Methodist Church

"As a church planter, I've learned far more from my failures than I have from my successes. Christian offers all of us, from the veteran pastor to the new church planter, a much-needed reminder that we all fail and that learning from those failures is the key to our future. From maintaining perspective to living through disappointment to picking yourself up and trying again, these are lessons we all learn. You can do it the hard way, or you can read this book!"

—Matt Miofsky, Founding and Lead Pastor,
The Gathering, St. Louis

Other Titles in Path 1's
Wesleyan Church Planting Resources Series

Vital Merger: A New Church Start Approach that Joins Church Families Together, (Foreword by Douglas T. Anderson); Fun & Done Press, 2013

A Missionary Mindset: What Church Leaders Need to Know to Reach Their Community—Lessons from E. Stanley Jones, by Douglas Ruffle; Discipleship Resources, 2016

Flipping Church: How Successful Church Planters Are Turning Conventional Wisdom Upside-Down, edited by Michael Baughman; Discipleship Resources, 2016

FAILING BOLDLY

HOW FALLING DOWN IN MINISTRY CAN BE THE START OF RISING UP

CHRISTIAN COON

Foreword by
REVEREND ROBERT SCHNASE
Bishop, United Methodist Church

DISCIPLESHIP
RESOURCES

ISBNs
978-0-88177-878-6 (print)
978-0-88177-879-3 (mobi)
978-0-88177-880-9 (ePub)

Library of Congress Control Number has been requested.

DR878

CONTENTS

SERIES PREFACE

PATH 1'S WESLEYAN CHURCH PLANTING RESOURCES

In Summer 2013, the staff of Path 1 (New Church Starts at Discipleship Ministries of The United Methodist Church), along with a selected group of associates from around the United States, embarked on an extensive "Road Trip." We visited more than 320 of the new churches planted in the previous five years. Through hundreds of conversations with church planters and judicatory leaders of congregational development, we learned about the hopes and heartaches of starting new places for new people and revitalizing existing churches among the people called Methodist in the United States. We learned about innovative "out of the box" church plants, as well as traditional strategies that are reaching new people and making disciples of Jesus Christ for the transformation of the world. We celebrated the many ways that annual conferences and districts of the church are finding to form new communities of faith. We also learned there was a lack of written resources available, which could guide new church planting in a Wesleyan theological perspective. Thus, we set out to create the Wesleyan Church Planting Resources. Our hope is that these resources will not only help those who plant new churches but also help revitalize existing churches.

Failing Boldly is the third book to be published as part of this initiative. Christian Coon, a co-founding pastor of the multi-site Urban Village Church in Chicago, Illinois, gives us a winsome story of how failure can lead to great and innovative ministry. Drawing from his experiences with Urban Village, Christian helps all of us learn the lessons of disappointment and failure for the sake of finding new and creative ways of relating to people in our midst with the good news of Jesus Christ.

Christian writes, "I believe that we lose out when we fail to examine failure because, however you define success, it usually comes as a result of stubbed toes, embarrassing missteps, and miscalculated risks."

How very true! I know you will find in these pages a delightful invitation to see failure in a whole new light and even, as Christian suggests, plan for it. I am grateful to Christian Coon's contribution to our series of books. I am sure you will be, too.

Douglas Ruffle
General Editor, Wesleyan Church Planting Resources

AUTHOR'S PREFACE

When you fold an 8½ x 11 piece of paper in half and set it on a table, it makes a nice little pup tent. The sides are nice and straight. The crease at the top is clean and crisp. You can put words on both sides for all the world to see. One summer evening in 2009, my friend Trey Hall and I created one of those paper tents. On one side, it said, "New Church for Chicago!" and we placed it proudly on a table inside a little Starbucks café, which was inside a large Barnes & Noble bookstore. Trey and I were a couple weeks into a rather daunting venture. We were full enough of ourselves (and hoping that we were also full enough of the Holy Spirit) to think we could start a new church in this great city that would, as we often said, "do church differently." It was a pretty audacious sentiment.

Church has been "done" for centuries so our attempt wasn't really all *that* different, but when attacking great ventures, deluding yourself into thinking that you're blazing new trails helps. If I waited to do something that was absolutely original and had never been attempted before, I would never have started anything. I did realize that we *were* starting something new in this particular place and at this particular time.

We put a notice on Meetup.com about an informal gathering of this new church at this Barnes & Noble on the corner of State & Jackson and thought, surely, we would overwhelm this store with hordes of people who had been hungering for just what we were offering. A few minutes passed and no one showed up. People are just getting off work, we told ourselves, and then more than a few minutes went by. No responses. One man did show up, and we had a nice conversation, but I also was looking out of the corner of my eye to see if others would stop by. They didn't. The staff at the Starbucks could rest easy that there would be no danger of exceeding their seating capacity. As the evening went along, our little paper tent, as all paper tents do, started to sag, and as we got up to leave, it was nearly flat, as were my hopes for a grand kick-off to this new venture.

Thankfully, things have gone better since then. A few people heard about us and word got out and we cobbled together enough interested people to launch worship for this new thing that we called Urban Village Church the following March. Since then, we've started three additional worshiping locations, and we seemed to have found a niche in the city with this way of doing church and sharing the love of God and neighbor.

But I am not writing this book to tell you how great things are. I have many church-growth books on my bookshelf and numerous three-ring binders in my closet from conferences that share secrets to church success. I have gone to seminars where a polished speaker has the great ProPresenter™ presentation and spells out steps that one can follow so that you, too, can EXPERIENCE AMAZING GROWTH IN YOUR CHURCH!

While occasionally helpful, I have grown a little weary of those books, conferences, and seminars. I often walk away from them feeling depressed and discouraged. What I'd love to know, Polished Church-Growth Speaker, is what happens when you *don't* succeed? Talk about your screw-ups and your missteps. Tell me how you failed because then I find you eminently more relatable. It's difficult for me to hear (and follow) your steps to success if you don't share a bit of your humanity with me. (Which may be a key reason why so many have been drawn to Christianity—God sharing God's humanity with us!)

As I thought about this book and discerned different ways of writing it, that theme of failure kept coming to mind. I've been a pastor since 1997, and one thing that has always been true is whenever I preach about my foibles and ways in which I fall short, people respond positively. Folks want to know that they're not the only ones who have doubts and travel down wayward paths. They want to know that they are not the only ones who fail. I hate to trot out the "Misery loves company" aphorism, but knowing that you're not the only one who has fallen flat on your face is strangely encouraging.

So this book is not really about success. I will not give you Five Reasons Why You Must Start a Multi-Site Church or Ten Steps to Reach Millennials. This book is about failure. Or, rather, this book highlights ways that churches (including ours) have failed. It also takes a look at how failure is a part of our faith; how there are numerous examples of biblical characters who are now forever memorialized in stained glass but didn't get things right at first. Later in their lives, however, they realized that God was able to further God's movement of grace and love through their failures.

But before you think, "Why would I read something that may be full of discouragement and despair?" I want to assure you I offer hope and encouragement, too. I'll talk about failure, yes, but also how failure is a springboard to new experiences and, hopefully, a deeper connection to God and what it means to be a leader in the church. I do not want you, church leader, to read this book and try to be Urban Village Church or Christian Coon. I do hope that reading it gives you the courage to fail. By that I mean, I hope that if fear of failure is one of the reasons you're not attempting something different in your context (regardless of whether it's cutting edge or not), maybe reading how others have failed and survived gives you the nudge to experiment and, if you're lucky, fall flat on your face.

Why would failing make you lucky? That's what we'll explore. In the first chapter, I start by defining failure and giving an overview of how we understand success and failure in the church. Sadly, there are so many reports about the failures and decline of the mainline church, leaders have either shrugged their shoulders and not done anything to respond, or they so fear failure that they frantically and frenetically grab at the next big cure-all that will bring success. I won't get into why things have "failed" (there are plenty of other books about that), but I want to explore why failure has defined and paralyzed the church and stopped it from taking risks.

What helps us respond to failure is being reminded of one of the core foundations of our faith: God's love for us, which I write about in the second chapter. This never, ever changes, and I think sometimes leaders don't let this become fully integrated into their lives. United Methodists, when reading about John Wesley's Aldersgate experience, focus on the "heart strangely warm'd" phrase, but another part of that confession also inspires me. A few words later Wesley wrote: "An assurance was given me that (Jesus) had taken away *my* sins, even *mine*." It's that "even mine" phrase that I love. We hear phrases like "Christ takes away my sins" or "God loves me," but it's that moment when we let that sink in (even mine! even me!) that is life changing. Too often, Christians get their sense of meaning from external sources rather than believing that God's grace and love are sufficient. We cannot fail/risk until we fully let that grace and love become part of who we are.

Lots of books highlight successful biblical characters (I'm looking at you, Jabez), but it's important to consider how the Bible not only includes but *highlights* failure. That's the third chapter. Exploring sacred stories (like the parable of the sower, Zechariah's response to an angel, and, of course, numerous hiccups from the disciples) help us realize that even "holy" people took some wrong turns and experienced frustration.

After we've established that failure is OK (even encouraged), it's important to share some how-to steps. Chapter 4 is Failure 101. Here's where we discuss steps you might take to integrate risk, innovation, and failure into church life and share some examples of how Urban Village and other churches are living this out.

We must recognize, though, that failure can be crippling (I speak from first-hand experience), which we explore in Chapter 5. It's one thing to know how to integrate failure into church life, but we must also know how to respond in those moments when opening up a food truck seems like a great career option because *anything* would be better than the mess at your church. I've had plenty of moments where I lament in my journal that nothing I'm doing is right and why on earth would God want me to do what I'm doing and maybe I should have stayed in that summer job where I sold children's shoes after all. In grace-filled moments, though, God speaks and reminds me that failure isn't final. And that I don't have the patience to horn kids' feet into shoes.

Finally, is it possible that failure can have benefits? Chapter 6 explores these possibilities including how faith, hope, perseverance, patience, and hospitality can all be "fruits of failure."

A word about the stories you see throughout the book. As a way to emphasize that *everyone* fails, I've asked some friends and colleagues to share brief anecdotes of times when things didn't go quite as well as they would have liked. I hope you can relate to them as much as I have.

My hope as you read this book is that at some point, God gives you the courage to try something new and risky in your context. As I noted earlier, I won't give you too many examples of what those might be because it's important that **you** are the one who come up with the idea and execute it; hopefully, with some other friends or colleagues in your community of faith. Failure is a lot more fun when done with others.

So pull out a piece of paper. Fold it in half. Write "Fail Boldly" on one side. As it begins to sag, prop it up again or stick it on a wall as a reminder that, in the words from a scene in the movie *Apollo 13,* "Failure is not an option!" I wholeheartedly agree.

It's a necessity.

———

While there are many stories of failure in this book, one thing at which I have succeeded is surrounding myself with wonderful friends, colleagues, and loved ones who have helped immensely in the writing of this book.

A very big thank you to Doug Ruffle, Candace Lewis, and the whole staff at Path 1 (the church-planting arm of The United Methodist Church) for giving me the opportunity to go through with this venture. Because I have a background in journalism, I thought writing this book wouldn't be that difficult of a task. Let's just say I failed in that assumption. Doug's encouragement has been vital, as have the insights of Paul Nixon, a New Church Strategist for Path 1. In addition to the many other hats he wears, Paul has been the coach for Trey Hall and myself since the very beginning of Urban Village. I'm also grateful to my editor in this process, Beth Gaede. Like any good teacher or coach, she was patient, firm, and pushed for something deeper within me.

Before I say thank you to all of my Urban Village colleagues, I want to acknowledge the good people of Riverside United Methodist Church in Riverside, Illinois, and Christ United Methodist Church in Deerfield, Illinois. These were my first two appointments, and the members there taught me so much about ministry, all the while supporting and stretching me. I'm also grateful to many Northern Illinois Conference colleagues, who supported and continue to support the vision of Urban Village, including those with whom I have worked the closest: Bishop Hee-Soo Jung, Bishop Sally Dyck, Martin Lee, James Preston, and Tracy Smith Malone.

Obviously this book wouldn't have happened without the patience and support of so many past and present staff colleagues at Urban Village Church, especially Brittany Isaac, Emily McGinley, Emily Jones, Erin James-Brown, Grant Crusor, Hannah Kardon, Caleb Murphree, Dawnn Brumfield, Tyler Sit, Rich Havard, Tim Kim, Paul Hahm, Becky Criollo, Sarah Marie Young, Colby Beserra, Darren Calhoun, and many, many interns and other staff members. Thank you for being the most amazing ministry team to work with. In addition, I'm indebted to so many UVC laity who have taken a chance on a new church over these last few years and have served with faithfulness and zeal.

I'll always be grateful for my parents, Rev. Dennis Coon and Jo Tsistinas, and the sacrifices they've made and love they've shown over the years. My brother Corey's presence in my life has always kept me grounded, for which I'm thankful. I don't know if there are many people who have an extended family—cousins, aunts, uncles, grandparents—as strong as mine, and I have never taken that for granted.

A preacher really can't be a preacher without stories, and the stories that are my two children—Caroline and Ethan—are priceless. Every parent is biased, of course, but, seriously, I've got great kids. Really great kids. You should meet them.

What can I say about Trey Hall? I simply can't describe what he has done for me. It has been a blessing to be his brother in Christ, close confidante, receiver of hilarious observations and text messages, and, of course, co-dreamer of the kind of church that *should* start in Chicago and that actually *has*.

As I think about pivotal moments (and failures) in my life where I have broken down into tears, it is my wife, Anne, who has always been strong, present, loving, and *there*. I have a memory of us—engaged but not yet married—riding in a car, talking about our future and the myriad possibilities. I think I said something about going into the ministry, and we both laughed because we knew that would never happen. And yet she's still with me today, adding untold color to my life and ministry. This book is for her.

FOREWORD

In 1995, I was serving my sixth year as pastor of First Church, McAllen, and we had a long-term strategic plan that we were pursuing with enthusiasm and success. Attendance had doubled, evangelism was flourishing, mission was thriving. We had remodeled our historic facilities and were actively seeking more space for parking. We negotiated for a piece of property, the lynchpin for further growth, and in March, we shook hands on the deal.

Two days, later the property owner backed out. I was devastated, as were the leaders of the congregation. Our future viability was at stake. Now the most we could hope for was to maintain ministries at current levels. On the same day, my father-in-law died unexpectedly. In the midst of our family crisis, a close friend lost her battle with breast cancer.

The road ahead, that for me had always seemed brightly lit, was now dark with grief and discouragement. What did the futility of the strategic plan mean for the church? Had I led them down the wrong course? I began to re-examine my call. I wondered if I really belonged in pastoral ministry. I felt like a failure because I could not see a way forward for the church now that the strategic plan was no longer valid. For two months, I stewed in a sense of defeat.

In May, the Trustees met for lunch. The mood was grim. The chairperson talked through the failed property deal in solemn tones. Nobody commented or asked questions. People picked at the food on their plates, eyes cast down, unable to think of a word that would relieve the disappointment. Gone was the energetic spirit that usually marked our conversations. I felt as hopeless as everyone else. Our carefully crafted plan for the future was now history.

After several moments of labored silence, a woman broke through the gloom with an unexpected comment. "This is not about the parking. Or the property. Or the strategic plan. This is about facing the fact that we have out-grown this facility. We don't have room for our children, for our worship, for our mission work." Someone else spoke up, "If we were serious about reaching young people, we'd be talking about soccer fields and not just parking lots." Another jumped in, "My own parents can't attend here because this building isn't accessible to the elderly." Another described what everyone was realizing, "God is calling us to think about something we never dared to talk about. The long-term future of our church is somewhere else."

To my utter amazement, an animated discussion ensued about relocating the congregation. One positive comment spontaneously followed another in quick succession, all of them energized by hope and passion. By the end of the meeting, the Trustees voted to recommend a feasibility study. Five months later, after careful analysis and much prayer, the church voted overwhelmingly to relocate. The Spirit moved through the congregation as we came to a new vision of our future. We set out to build a faithful, welcoming, mission-focused, bi-cultural church that would serve the community for generations to come. An imagined desolate future became shot through with possibilities.

Seven years later, we moved into 60,000 square feet of buildings designed in the same Spanish Romanesque as our downtown facility, but positioned on seventeen acres at a major intersection. Attendance doubled again, and we received nearly 200 new members during the first two years after relocation, one third of whom were Hispanic.

The failure of the original strategic plan was a painful but necessary experience in order for us to see options we otherwise never would have considered. We became a different church because of the loss and grief of 1995. I became a different pastor.

I could recount dozens of other failures along my journey— Bible studies that start strong and then fizzle out; new worship services that launch with great fanfare, then die away; mission projects that bring unintended consequences; financial campaigns that fall short; leadership teams that bear tremendous fruit and then spiral into conflict; youth programs that draw a crowd but never form into a ministry. Even in growing churches, more initiatives fail than succeed. Learning to fail successfully is an important skill for ministry.

Jesus tells the Parable of the Sower to relieve the discouragement of his disciples and to make us more failure-tolerant. The seeds we cast get swallowed up by birds, scorched by sunlight, and choked by weeds, but nevertheless a harvest comes forth in lives changed by the grace of God. It matters to God that we keep sowing despite our perceived failures.

How can we make failure our friend? Christian Coon, in *Failing Boldly: How Falling Down in Ministry Can be the Start of Rising Up,* provides insight and encouragement to Christian leaders on how to integrate risk, innovation, and failure into ministry. He invites us to embrace failure as normative and necessary, as a feature of ministry that teaches patience, deepens humility, sharpens skills, and binds us to one another. Failure strengthens our reliance upon God.

No other book directs our attention toward failure as necessary for faithful ministry. Read *Failing Boldly* to prompt yourself and your church toward greater boldness for Christ. The book helps us navigate the spiritual hazards to otherwise constrain us or derail us from our mission. Coon gives us the courage to lead without becoming paralyzed by the gnawing fear of failure.

Reverend Robert Schnase
Bishop, United Methodist Church
Author, *Five Practices of Fruitful Congregations* and
Just Say Yes! Unleashing People for Ministry.

1

TAKING A FRESH LOOK
AT FAILURE

It was the cross that signified that I had truly failed. Or, more accurately, the Red Cross.

It should have been a day of great celebration and accomplishment. I was running the Boston Marathon, which is on the Running Bucket List of many who lace up their shoes and dare to complete twenty-six miles. I ran cross-country and track in high school and a year of cross-country in college so I have always been a pretty decent runner. I ran a personal best in the Columbus Marathon (Ohio) in 2003, and the time qualified me for Boston. Unfortunately in my training leading up to Boston, I had an Achilles heel injury, which set my training back, but I wasn't going to let this opportunity pass me by. I would just scale my pace back a bit. *Enjoy* the race, rather than worrying about my time. That worked pretty well for the first sixteen miles, but as soon as I entered Mile 17, my legs and brain started conspiring against me:

> *Legs: You do know you haven't properly trained for this, right?*
> *Brain: You and your "I'll just enjoy the race and not worry about my time" attitude.*
> *Legs: You realize you still have ten miles to go, right?*
> *Brain: Let's just take your Boston Marathon t-shirt, drop out, and call it a day. Even getting this far is an accomplishment.*

Feelings of exhaustion and pain come over most marathoners at some point (it's known as "The Wall"), but usually I can battle through those feelings. This wall was different and hit me earlier than normal. At the sixteen-mile mark, I started running 50 percent of the time and walking the other 50 percent. With each mile, that ratio shifted more and more toward the walking component until around Mile 22, I was spent. I saw the Red Cross tent and walked over and slumped into a chair. Some very kind medical professionals came over and checked on me, but I don't remember much of my conversation with them, other than their insistence that I drink more water. All I could see was hundreds of people passing me by. My brain had another message for me.

Whereas before it was telling me to drop out, that I'd already accomplished something, it now had a different story: *You have failed. You have failed. You have failed.*

Hearing Voices

I don't think I'm alone in hearing that internal voice. It seems to pop up in the minds of many who strive to accomplish something, whether it's running a marathon or succeeding in one's vocation, including my profession, church leadership.

Those unfamiliar with the inner workings of the church may assume that pastoral leaders are immune to self-criticism and feelings of failure. After all, doesn't a pastor have a sense of divine inner peace that repels these kinds of thoughts? I think many pastors would respond, "If only . . ."

No, church leaders hear those internal voices just as much as anyone. Why are my worship numbers declining? Why is the financial giving dropping off? Is it just me, or do my sermons seem really flat? Why haven't I been able to get through to my congregation? What is wrong with me? Why did I fail?

When I decided to write a book a couple years ago, I knew what the book would *not* be about: church growth. I've read many of those kinds of books and some have been helpful, but, as I noted in the introduction, a part of me feels a little depressed after reading them. I liken it to auditioning for a role in a play and then discovering the next person auditioning is Meryl Streep. You thought you were pretty good, but compared to a *real* success, maybe you're not so great after all.

Instead, I wanted to write an anti-church growth book. I wanted to write about failure. It's such a harsh word, *failure.* There's a finality to it and with that finality comes a stigma that doesn't easily leave one's psyche. That stigma also brings with it a nice dose of loneliness, which amplifies the internal voice that leads us to believe we are the only ones who have ever failed.

I'm happy to report that all of us fail, even those who seem to be "successes." In his book *Born Losers: A History of Failure in America,* Scott A. Sandage highlights numerous examples of notable Americans who did not always achieve success nor always receive affirmation. Sandage opens his book by describing a funeral held in May 1862. Typically, a funeral will have its share of stories about the deceased's goodness, but one eulogizer at this particular funeral took a different track. He focused on the dead man's unfulfilled potential. "He seemed born for greatness . . . and I cannot help counting it a fault in him that he had no ambition."[1] The eulogizer? Ralph Waldo Emerson. The person he was speaking of? Henry David Thoreau. Emerson apparently desired more from Thoreau and considered it a disappointment and failure of sorts that Thoreau didn't meet those expectations. (I have to believe that as Emerson was speaking, a few people made mental notes: Don't invite Mr. Emerson to speak at my funeral).

Ralph may have been a little harsh on his friend Henry, but this story exemplifies that no one—even a person you and I would consider a "success"—is immune to the perceptions of others, which, in turn, can have an impact on our sense of failure. Americans love success stories. Our most common form of communication these days—social media—is built on the premise that we show our *best* side so that we look successful to our peers, whether we know them well or not. Churches and denominations love success stories, too. We hear so often about the declining influence of religion in society that we hunger for a word about something that's going well.

But I believe that we lose out when we fail to examine failure because, however you define success, it usually comes as a result of stubbed toes, embarrassing missteps, and miscalculated risks. Indeed, history is replete with notable individuals who failed at one point or another.

In 1907 there was a boy who was born to an upper middle-class family that wanted for nothing. As the boy grew up, he developed a sunny personality, and it also became clear that he was very smart. He excelled in school and perhaps family members assumed he would follow in his father's footsteps and teach at a collegiate level. But the boy had a different vocation in mind. He had a hunger for learning about issues of faith. At age thirteen, in fact, he declared that he would be a theologian and was dedicated to following that path. He earned his doctorate when he was only twenty-one. At twenty-eight, he took two part-time jobs, including becoming a chaplain at a university near his home. His attempts to reach the students, however, did not start well. He put up flyers to promote a theological discussion group, but someone kept tearing them down. He tried hosting lectures, prayer services, and Bible studies. When he arrived with hope at the time and place of his first discussion group, he waited. And waited. And waited. No one showed up. Morning devotions that he tried to lead? Canceled for lack of demand. There was one exception. A fraternity said they'd agree to have a discussion about ecclesiology on two conditions. One, that they could meet at a local beer hall. And, two, that the budding theologian/chaplain would pick up the tab. Not a great start to ministry. This hopeful faith leader? Dietrich Bonhoeffer.

One more example. Growing up, Phil Vischer was both wowed with advances in video and technology and, as a Christian, also troubled that mainstream media was dominated by the likes of Madonna videos. He had a dream that he felt was God-inspired to compete with major media corporations by creating smart and funny forms of entertainment that would appeal to people of all ages, while also communicating a message of God's love. He saw the potential of computer-generated graphics and, after years of borrowing money and trying to create different characters and stories, he came up with a concept that may have had a few people scratching their heads. Talking vegetables? Yes, answered Phil. Bob the Tomato and Larry the Cucumber, to be exact.

Veggie Tales, of course, quickly became a huge success, selling millions of videos and setting Phil on the path toward fulfilling what he thought was a Spirit-filled vision. He allowed this vision to become grander and more audacious. He hired more people for his company, Big Idea Productions. Big Idea's revenues went from

$1.3 million in 1996 to $44 million in 1999. His vision, however, soon outgrew his reality. The company grew too quickly and made too many incorrect revenue projections and, in 2003, it declared bankruptcy. If you've failed, you're in excellent company.

Despite the fact that *everyone* has failed, when we go through failure ourselves, it feels as if we're the *only* one who experiences it. What makes failure even more visible and visceral in our society today is that everything is so public. Even the word "fail" has become more powerful. A 2009 *New York Times* article highlighted the fact that "fail" used to be a simple verb meaning being unsuccessful or falling short of expectations.[2] That seemed to change in the early 00s. The *Times* article pointed to an Urbandictionary.com post in 2003 that said that fail could also be used as an interjection, some verbal salt to pour into a person's (or your own) wound. Some examples from a recent search I made of "#fail" on Twitter: One person was chagrined that he couldn't use a credit card at the London City Airport (#fail), another failed to bring an umbrella with her even when the forecast said it would rain (#fail), and one person even tweeted out a #fail at a sunset! (Apparently it wasn't as vivid as the tweeter wanted).

The *Times* article continued: "In a few years' time, the use of *fail* as an interjection caught on to such an extent that particularly egregious objects of ridicule required an even stronger barb: *major fail*, *überfail*, *massive fail* or, most popular of all, *epic fail*. The intensifying adjectives hinted that *fail* was becoming a new kind of noun: not simply a synonym for *failure* but, rather, a derisive label to slap on a miscue that is eminently mockable in its stupidity or wrongheadedness."[3]

Ironically, even "failure" itself can't escape a sense of failure. The Wikipedia page of the word "failure" notes at the top that, "This article was considered for deletion, and requires cleanup according to the discussion. Please improve this article if you can; the deletion discussion may suggest necessary improvements."

But despite the fact that individuals (like Phil Vischer) and entities (like Wikipedia) all go through failure so publicly, it still stings when we go through it ourselves. For church leaders, the potential for failure to be more than a sting is significant.

When Church Leaders Fail

As I noted earlier, church leaders struggle with failure as well. I became a church planter several years ago, and one of my support systems was (and still is) a Facebook group called Progressive Church Planters. It's a great place to share ideas, but it has also become a place to be vulnerable. Some recent posts:

"This whole thing can be just heartbreaking."
"Sometimes being missional sucks . . ."
". . . we just lost financial and Cabinet support . . ."
"It sucks when people leave your church."
". . . rough day . . ."

It's challenging enough to be a church leader in the twenty-first century, but it's particularly potent when you compare yourself with peers who are seemingly doing well. It may bring back memories of high school when you did poorly on a test and then you looked across the aisle at a classmate's paper and noticed a bright shiny "A" with stars dancing around it. When you looked back at your test and saw your less-than-desirable grade with no stars, your head dropped and you asked, "What's wrong with me? Why did I fail?" (I'm not alone in having this memory, am I?)

That feeling that you have when you're young doesn't leave when you get older. You might attend church-growth conferences and then hear about the successes of other churches and it seems to *come so easy to them*. Or maybe your supervisor recommends the latest church-growth book, and you think, here, here are all the answers, but you find yourself reading through it and instead of feeling inspired, you experience anxiety and added pressure. The formula of church growth may not work either.

I have no way to measure this, and I may be biased since I'm a church leader myself, but it seems like adding God to the list of people you've failed ramps up the potential for deep discouragement. If things aren't measuring up in your church, not only are you feeling like you're not doing your job well, but there may also be a sense that you're letting down your parishioners and perhaps

---

At least fifteen to twenty law students from nearby SMU studied on a daily basis at Union—the coffee shop and new church start that I lead. A couple of them even came to worship with us on Tuesday nights. Our law school customers and worship attendees were loyal, but only made up a fraction of how many we could connect with. We launched a big event to raise awareness about Union on campus.

We orchestrated a combination we were sure no law student could turn down: A panel of partners from nearby law firms, free Pabst Blue Ribbon, and free Peanut Butter and Jelly Sandwiches.

We prepared for the multitudes and publicized like crazy: PBR, PBJ & Partners. Who could resist? Apparently the entire student body.

The nearby homeless shelter got a lot of PB&J, and I was drinking PBR for months.

Lesson learned: PBR pairs nicely with PB&J. You should try it.

—Mike Baughman
Founding Pastor & Community Curator, Union Coffee
Author, *Flipping Church*

---

some denominational official or supervisor, and, here's the kicker, you're disappointing God. We feel a bit like the servant in the parable of the talents (Matthew 25:14-30) who buried his one talent rather than multiplied it and then had to sheepishly confess what he had (or, rather, hadn't) done. We may know that we did our best to multiply our ministry like our contemporaries, but why is it that they seem to double their "talents" and we seemingly have nothing to show for ours?

Many of us start our ministries on high notes and with grand expectations. For an ordained pastor, the ordination service can feel like the pinnacle, like a wedding can be the pinnacle of a marriage. I was ordained a probationary deacon in The United Methodist Church in 1995, and that ordination service still has an indelible impact on my identity. I wasn't sure I wanted to go into local-church ministry when I got ordained. I had an interest in combining journalism and religion and had started a double master's degree program that would conceivably allow me to pursue both of these fields. There was this nagging feeling, though, that I should also keep going with the ordination process. I told the committee that approved me for that initial ordination that I wasn't completely sure what I wanted to do, but I didn't share with them that one of the reasons I was going through the ordination process was, well, you know, "just in case" I changed my mind about journalism. Not exactly a "Here I am, send me" Isaiah moment, but many of us come to ministry through the backdoor.

Something changed in me during the actual ordination, however. At the time, I belonged to the Iowa Conference of the UMC, and the bishop was Charles Wesley Jordan. The probationary deacons lined up before going onto the dais, and we solemnly made our way across and knelt down at kneelers with our names placed in front of us. I can't recall what I was thinking before the bishop stood in front of me, but I'll never forget the moment he laid his strong hands on my shoulders. I have a photograph of me looking up at the bishop, and the look on my face is almost unrecognizable. If I've ever had a time when my face shone because of an experience with the holy, this was it.

The liturgy that the bishop used in that ordination service read, "(Name), take authority as a deacon in the Church to preach the Word of God, and to serve all God's people." All I remember are the first few words. Bishop Jordan intoned, "Christian . . . Trevor . . . Coon . . . Take Au-THOR-iteee . . ." He put such a strong emphasis on that second syllable of "authority" any hesitation or self-doubt I had about going into the ministry was completely wiped away in that moment. Of course, that feeling of invincibility faded as I did the work of actual ministry and was in a setting where people looked to me as a professional religious person (my typical inner response in these situations was, "Who am I to be a/your pastor?").

But that day in June 1995 was powerful, as evidenced by my tears afterward. I see that same look of awe and invincibility every year at our annual gathering of United Methodists when I clap and cheer for our new ordinands as they stand before all of us. They are ready to live into this powerful calling and, if they're all like I was, they believe wholeheartedly, "I can do this! Nothing can stop me! God is with me!"

In many ways, church leaders (clergy and laity) need moments like these to affirm their countercultural decision to follow Jesus instead of societal norms. But I think those same leaders also have moments of wondering whether that moment of literal glory was all a set-up.

Because we feel these experiences (like an ordination service) so personally, because we feel that God has intimately and thoughtfully chosen *us* to tackle ministry, when we experience hardship in a vocation into which we feel called, it's hard not to take that personally, as well. We may second-guess our calling ("Maybe God *didn't* choose me . . . maybe I shouldn't be in the ministry after all"), or we may feel like we're bad listeners, that we're not following the guidance that God has given to us.

In the next chapter, I'll go into more detail about what was a pivotal moment in Jesus' ministry: his baptism, when he came up out of the Jordan River and a voice from the heavens affirmed his son-ship. Right after that stunning moment, he immediately went into the wilderness to be tempted, and I have to believe there was at least one moment in the first few of those forty days when Jesus wondered, "What the hell happened?" It can be a tough fall when you're at the mountaintop and quickly plummet to the valley.

Paul had a similar experience. Many of us are familiar with his Damascus conversion. In Acts 9:17, Ananias confirms Paul's (who was Saul at the time) calling and tells him, "Brother Saul, the Lord Jesus, who appeared to you on your way here, has sent me so that you may regain your sight and be filled with the Holy Spirit." Scales fall from Saul's eyes, his sight is restored, he is baptized, he eats a good meal, and he begins to "proclaim Jesus."

A few verses later, however, we read, "After some time had passed, the Jews plotted to kill him" (Acts 9:23). Again, I wonder if Saul thought to himself, "What the hell is happening? I went from being filled with the Holy Spirit and following the call to proclaim Jesus and now I have people who literally want to kill me! Did I misinterpret the vision I received? Am I failing in not doing what Jesus expected of me?"

Obviously I'm reading between the lines here, but it gives me some comfort to think that Jesus and Paul may have wondered why they experienced hardship so early in their ministries? Had they misinterpreted God's vision for them? Clearly Jesus and Paul made it through the hardships, but it's not so easy for us non-Jesus and non-Paul types to persevere. For the rest of us, moving from

11

heavenly affirmation to hellish discouragement is a little like finally climbing up the ladder to the high dive, admiring the view and then attempting to do a flip before flailing wildly, landing on your back, and enduring the laughter of peers (not that this happened to me when I was eight and it's still a vivid memory or anything).

I don't think it's a coincidence that the end of Isaiah 43:1 says, "I have called you by name, you are mine," and then verse 2 notes that *when* (not if) we pass through the waters and rivers, and *when* we walk through the fire, God will be with us, and we will not be consumed by the flames. Ministry takes us through the high of being called by name and the low of feeling like we're drowning or being burned . . . and often both can happen within the same day. We need the glory of something like an ordination or laying on hands or voice from the clouds in order to do something as audacious as be the hands, feet, and voice of God. Who in their right mind does this?

But after we muster up the courage to say yes to this calling, ministry can set us up for a hard fall when (not if) we fail. How so? When we fail, there may be a feeling that we've disappointed God or others whom we want to please or impress. A congregation might have been told that things will get better when the new pastor shows up, so that church is expecting big things and we don't want to let them down. A denominational supervisor may be watching closely and making mental notes if a church doesn't turn around quickly, and we don't want negative reports to go in our personnel files. These pressures can be heavy, which is probably why leaders turn to a passage like Matthew 11:28-30: "Come to me, all you that are weary and are carrying heavy burdens, and I will give you rest. Take my yoke upon you, and learn from me; for I am gentle and humble in heart, and you will find rest for your souls. For my yoke is easy, and my burden is light."

Of course, everyone, no matter what they do for a living, feels the weight of expectation, but it feels a little heavier to those whose identity is so tied up in their vocation. We invest our lives into this. For church leaders, when you add the fact that it's *a calling from God*, that adds another layer of complication, and it may make it a bit more difficult to shake things off when you fail. Larry Sonner has been listening to clergy for forty years and can attest to the struggle of living up to this calling.

Larry is a retired pastoral counselor who served in the Iowa Conference of The United Methodist Church and has heard thousands of clergy share their the burdens and anxieties. He senses a difference in how clergy experience their vocations compared to how others might view their jobs. "It's easier for people in other vocations to say in their minds, 'To heck to giving myself to this. It's just a job.' Clergy have a lot harder time doing this, if they can do it at all," he says.[4]

When you wear a collar or when people call you Reverend Smith or Pastor Maria, it's very easy for your job to consume your total identity. If your sole way of identifying yourself is through your vocation, when failure comes, the next easy conclusion to make is that *you* are a failure, too.

What makes this dynamic even more complicated is that we live in a time where, more than ever, clergy are seemingly set up to feel like they're failures. There are instances where we can blame certain individuals for this set-up (like denominational officials or local church leaders or other pastoral leaders themselves), but there are no easy scapegoats. The decline of the mainline church has ramped up the anxiety for many, and that often produces higher and, at times, unrealistic expectations. I'll spare you pages and pages of data about this decline, but here's the obligatory hat tip to the numbers.

The Pew Research Center's latest Religious Landscape Study, done in 2014, showed that there were an estimated 36 million mainline Protestant adults in the United States, a drop from 41 million in 2007.[5] Another way to look at this is that 14.7 percent of U.S. adults are mainline Protestants, compared to 18.1 percent in 2007. All this despite overall U.S. population growth. What may also heighten a sense of failure among professional church leaders is that, despite the decline of membership, there's an upswing in the number of clergy. This probably doesn't help clergy if they're feeling a sense of decline and failure, and they sense that there are other clergy who are also anxiously looking for work. In a June 2015 blog post, Tobin Grant of the Religion News Service noted that, "over the last half of the 20th century the number of mainline clergy increased year after year. It has only been over the past decade or so that the number of clergy has leveled."[6]

So what are we to do? How do churches and denominations respond? And are these reactions adequate to this decline and failure to reach new generations? Whether it's intentional or not, I fear that the pressure to turn things around quickly has created an environment where leaders are expected to try ministries that don't fit their contexts and where denominations are quick to pull the plug on failed ministry experiments without enough thought about the blood, sweat, and tears that clergy have invested.

Many pastors have experienced this scenario: A pastor is called or appointed to a church, and someone (e.g. a denominational official or a local church leader) who seemingly knows more than they do describes this new ministry as a diamond in the rough. Even though the church has shown decades of decline and/or may be in an area that has gone through significant cultural change, the new setting is painted as prime for growth explosion.

You're just the leader to turn this church around, the new pastor might be told. *There are all kinds of potential here. It's a gold mine of gospel opportunity. It's just waiting to explode.*

Again, I trust that this is all done out of a sense of encouragement, but what it also may do is set the new pastor up for unrealistic expectations. Rather than being told the hard but necessary truth about this new position, the pastor may find herself thinking she's entering a situation that will bring her vocational satisfaction and allow her to have significant societal impact.

During the first few weeks or months in this church, however, she soon realizes that this situation may not quite be the ugly-duckling-on-the-verge-of-becoming-a-swan that she thought it was or, rather, was told it was. She discovers there are reasons why the church is in decline, but she's determined and so she engages in significant community outreach. She introduces new and creative worship. She starts a new and relevant Bible study. Nothing seems to work, and she finds herself waking up in the middle of the night wondering, *why is nothing working? Why am I failing? I was told that this was a gold mine of gospel opportunity!*

It's easy to place blame on a denominational official in this scenario, but these officials feel the weight of failure, too. They want to believe there is a lot of potential out there. They want to believe in their pastors. But it is challenging to face reality and even more difficult to be honest about it. Indeed, officials may get criticized by clergy if they *are* painfully honest because the church—both laity and clergy—want to believe there is no ministerial roadblock that can't be overcome. After all, doesn't Philippians remind us that we can do all things in Christ who strengthens us?

We all respond to these challenges in different ways. I've noticed at least three responses, which are to model others (copying Hero Pastors), tune everything out and do business as usual (becoming Lukewarm Pastors), or simply put in more and more hours (defaulting to Workaholic Pastors).

Copying Hero Pastors

Every denomination has them; it's hard not to hold them up as saviors. They are the faithful, creative, tireless pastors, who started or turned around a church and now lead worship services attended by thousands, write numerous books, and speak at countless conferences. It's hard not to get swept up in the Hero Pastor hysteria because there's a reason they've been successful. They're very good at what they do! Their books are interesting, their talks/sermons are engaging, and stories of how their success began are often compelling. (Such origin stories often begin with the pastor starting a church in an unusual place or a pastor reviving a church when there were only a few people left).

The temptation is for denominational officials to have all their pastors read a Hero Pastor's book and use the information in the book to turn their own church around. Clergy fall into this trap on their own as well, even without others' encouragement. *If I just follow the Hero Pastor's steps one by one, I, too, will achieve success.* But following this formula rarely produces the same success, and, to be fair, many of the Hero Pastors I hear and read about tell their audience that they shouldn't expect to copy them. They encourage people to follow their principles but not necessarily their blueprint. It's hard to hear that message, though, because we want easy answers that give us simple directions that produce quick results.

By no means do I put myself in the "Hero Pastor" category, but I have had colleagues want to meet with me to hear about Urban Village. When I try to explain that there is no "secret sauce recipe" for success, I sense some disappointment in their responses.

Some denominational officials rue the fact that they have no Hero Pastors and subconsciously try to create them. Clergy try their best not to get caught up in Hero Pastor worship, but that, too, is hard to do, because the seeming fruits of success mean more vocational stability and notoriety from others, which can be difficult to resist. Denominational officials aren't the only ones who may not respond to failure in healthy ways. Clergy do it, too, and I have certainly compared myself plenty of times to Hero Pastors.

I served two United Methodist churches in the Chicago suburbs before starting Urban Village. The second of the two was in a suburb called Deerfield, where I made many wonderful relationships. There were a few couples in the church who were snowbirds, meaning they spent the spring and summer in the Deerfield area and then wintered in warmer climes. One of these couples lived in Florida in the winter and became active in a church there. After worship one summer morning, I was chatting with the husband of this couple and the topic of their Florida church came up. He was talking about how big it was, how many programs they had, and I found myself shifting from an attitude of, "How great that you've found a church home in Florida!" to "What's so great about *them*?" But the kicker was when he started talking about the Florida pastor's great sermons. Clearly (according to the snowbird's description) this was a Hero Pastor. The parishioner looked at me and in attempt to make me feel better . . . didn't. "Your sermons are good," he said. (That made me feel good). "But his sermons are *great*." (Not so good.)

I realize he said I was a "good" preacher, but, of course, I immediately transformed "good" into "mediocre." I found myself feeling aggravated and yet eager to find out why this pastor's sermons were so great. Was there something I could do to also be a great preacher, at least in this parishioner's eyes? Had I failed this parishioner with what were apparently just "meh" sermons?

When worship numbers are stagnant or declining, it's tempting to compare ourselves to Hero Pastors. Or at least it's hard to not be envious of them, and then we feel bad about that envy (a deadly sin!), which makes things worse.

We all know the story of David and Goliath, but we sometimes forget the verses that immediately precede the action. David has courageously offered to fight the giant Philistine ("Let no one's heart fail because of him; your servant will go and fight with this Philistine" [1 Samuel 17:32])—you know a guy means business when he speaks of himself in the third person). Saul protests that David is "just a boy," while Goliath is an experienced warrior, but David eventually convinces him. Saul wanted to help David so he clothed him with his armor. "David strapped Saul's sword over the armor, and he tried in vain to walk, for he was not used to them. Then David said to Saul, 'I cannot walk with these; for I am not used to them.' So David removed them" (1 Samuel 17:39).

How tempting it is for "ordinary" pastors to try on the armor of Hero Pastors! We see these clergy whose churches have doubled or tripled in size or they've written books or articles, and we believe that if we simply wear what they're wearing we will not fail. Admitting it doesn't usually work like that can be difficult.

During the summer before my senior year in college, I worked in the shoe department of a kids' clothing store. It actually wasn't that bad of a job until the last couple of weeks before I went back to college: back-to-school shopping season. One mother brought in her son for shoes, and the boy was convinced that he wanted soccer cleats for everyday wear because they looked cool (coolness being an important element of being seen as or emulating a hero). I assumed the mom would inform him that this wasn't practical, but she let him try the cleats on, and he started walking around the linoleum floors. Anyone could tell this wouldn't work. He slipped around a bit and walked awkwardly to the point where it was almost comical. After this trial run of staggering/walking, he looked at us both and pronounced, "They're perfect." (The mom then turned to me, the "expert," and gave me the dirty job of telling the boy that, no, you cannot wear soccer cleats to school.)

Sometimes pastors wear Hero Pastor armor (or soccer cleats) that doesn't fit, but they don't want to admit it because copying a successful pastor's success is supposed to be the quick fix to turn churches around. We should follow David's example, however.

David knew that the armor didn't fit and wouldn't allow him to fulfill his mission effectively. He took the next courageous step and said as much. *I cannot walk in these; for I am not used to them.* You may think I'm exaggerating a bit by using courageous as an adjective, but it's apt. We can try on another's armor, but it does take courage to admit that trying to emulate someone else's ministry doesn't and won't work.

David doesn't just end things there, though. After telling Saul that Saul's armor doesn't fit, he removes the armor, takes stock of what he does have (some stones and a sling), judges it to be adequate, and heads off to face the Philistine. For church leaders, admitting that another's armor doesn't fit, removing it, believing that what you have is enough, and then responding to your context with your own gifts is huge.

Giving into the Hero Pastor temptation, trying to be someone you're not, is an understandable response to a sense of failure. Another temptation is succumbing to being a Lukewarm Pastor.

Becoming a Lukewarm Pastor

I was blessed to be able to go on two pilgrimages to England in recent years, following in the footsteps of John and Charles Wesley. Not surprisingly, I've been rereading some of my old seminary textbooks on the Wesleys, in addition to making my way through an excellent new offering, *A Heart Strangely Warmed: John and Charles Wesley and their Writings,* edited by my friend Jonathan Dean. In addition to the inspirational nuggets one finds from John Wesley's writings (e.g. "Give me one hundred preachers who fear nothing but sin and desire nothing but God, and I care not a straw whether they be clergymen or laymen, such alone will shake the gates of hell and set up the kingdom of heaven on earth."),[7] I was also pleased to come across readings that convey a vulnerable John, too. One quote in particular caught me by surprise. This was from a letter written by John to an Anglican bishop: "To this day I have abundantly more temptation to lukewarmness than to impetuosity; to be saunterer *inter sylvas Academicas,* a philosophical sluggard, than an itinerant preacher. And, in fact, what I now do is so exceeding little, compared with what I am convinced I ought to do, that I am often ashamed before God . . ."[8]

It's interesting that John favored impetuosity over lukewarmness. He seemed to want emotion, rashness, impulsiveness. He worried about having a religion that focuses only on the mind and not the heart. One wouldn't think that a man as laser-focused as Wesley would have to worry about lukewarmness, but he wrote about this concern during the peak of his popularity.

Being lukewarm connotes a lack of passion. A shrug of the shoulders. Contentedness with adequacy. An automatic "meh" response when asked how things are going. A few church leaders may have had this feeling from the very beginnings of their ministry (and I'm guessing those folks aren't reading this book), but I have to believe that we fall into the Lukewarm Pastor category over time. Pastors who had zeal and passion when they first started in the ministry find that for various reasons—worship attendance decline, ill-fitting appointments or calls, loneliness, and a lack of appreciation for their own gifts could be a few culprits—the zeal and passion have been sapped. Instead of trying new things and risking, the pastors do just enough to keep the doors open and the remaining members content. Busy work takes up most of a Lukewarm Pastor's time, work that really doesn't advance the church.

Don't get me wrong, sometimes our minds and souls need a break, and so we engage in mindless tasks like organizing bookcases or cleaning out files. This also gives us a sense of accomplishment when we're not quite sure what strategic steps to take next or don't have the energy to accomplish much beyond the minimum. The problem arises when we engage in ministerial busy work as a way to avoid true risk, because being lukewarm usually means avoiding risk and, therefore, avoiding failure.

One of my temptations toward lukewarmness is to look over Urban Village's database of names. I go through the lists of people who haven't been active in a while, and I keep trying to figure out why they stopped engaging and what I can do to get them to come back to church. Again, there's nothing inherently wrong with this, but it usually doesn't move me (or our church) forward. There's comfort in trying to reengage people that you know (even though it also brings up memories of supposed failure because I also rehash and try to figure out if I did anything wrong to repel them in the first place), but it takes me away from thinking about how we can engage people who *aren't* a part of our community. I go to the people who are familiar to me.

One would think that after a few years of church planting, evangelism and engaging new people (strangers!) would feel as natural to me as sitting down to dinner with close friends. But I still have to push myself because it makes me uneasy and, yes, sets me up for awkward failures. I like to tell stories of street evangelism, where I come off as this charismatic yet humble servant of the Lord who can dazzle people with a few words of authentic conversation that convince them that they should give Jesus (and

Urban Village Church) a try. Those stories are in the minority. Instead, I have a lot of stories of me emailing, texting, and tweeting people who are or have been a part of the church at some point and usually getting no responses.

A sample e-mail: "Hey (insert name here), just wanted to check in and see how you were. We haven't seen you in a while so I hope you're well. Know that you're missed and looking forward to seeing you soon."

I've written a lot of those kinds of emails. They're fine things to do. I think the recipients appreciate receiving them and, occasionally, they do spur a person to reengage with the church. It's also a fairly safe activity. Yes, there's a decent chance that the person won't respond in the way I'd like (if the person responds at all), and I may wonder what I did that caused the person to detach from the community, but I'm not really risking anything. Spending time on social media can be a lukewarm activity, too, as we like and retweet certain things in the hope that it catches a person's attention. Or maybe we read a book or article that gives us some good information, but we never take the next step and act on these things. These kinds of activities may feel like we're doing something, but they're not likely to stoke our ministerial fires.

Robert Schnase is a bishop of the United Methodist Church and the author of numerous books, including *Five Practices of Fruitful Congregations*. Schnase doesn't use the term "lukewarm pastor," but he does note that there are competent pastors who may not stretch themselves because they'd rather keep their congregations happy.

"We as denominational leaders need to encourage these pastors to try new things without making them pay some huge penalty if these experiments don't go well," Schnase told me in an interview. "We need to protect the experimenters while keeping our standards of excellence and accountability."[9]

The danger of becoming a Lukewarm Pastor is that one just goes through the motions without increasing one's ministerial heart rate. At the opposite end of the spectrum is one other type of pastor who may believe that simply putting in more hours is the answer to decline.

Defaulting to Workaholic Pastor

Whether you try to mimic a Hero Pastor or succumb to the temptation of being mainly a Lukewarm Pastor, you may find that you're not getting the results you desire. And you're also not getting the results that a denominational official or lay leader desires either. The natural reaction to the anxiety of failing yourself and failing others (and failing God?) is to do what we're supposed to do as Americans. Try harder! Work longer hours!

I'm a Midwesterner so the try harder/work longer concept comes naturally for me. One summer while I was a college student (a couple of years before my shoe sales adventure), I worked in my hometown packing explosives for an explosives company. I always like dropping that job into conversations because it sounds so dangerous and makes me out to be a bit of a daredevil, but it was one of the most mundane (and safe) jobs I've ever had. I've never made sausage, but I imagine it was kind of like that. We worked in this hot trailer with the radio blaring all day, which is probably why I know the hit songs of 1987 by heart. Occasionally there'd be a little diversity in the job when we got to go to the company's storage facility and unload a shipment from a truck into storage.

One of the company's employees was a guy named Chuck. Chuck was a little cantankerous, and I could never seem to please him. Chuck also was a prodigious perspirer. I'm sure he broke out into a little sweat when he brushed his teeth in the morning. To him, sweating was a badge of honor, evidence that you were putting in a good day's work. I, on the other hand, did not sweat as much as Chuck did, and he loved to point this out.

"Are you even working? (Expletive), you're not even sweating!" he'd say to me often, and then he'd mumble something as he walked away. I felt shame when he uttered these comments, like I was letting down my hardworking Midwestern ancestors, so I'd try to lift more boxes and go even faster and pray that my pores would open up so that the sweat would come, and Chuck would say with pride, "Now there's a real worker!"

Many of us had a Chuck in our lives that made us feel like we weren't trying hard enough. Maybe you have one now! When our churches don't grow, a natural impulse is to go to even more conferences where a Hero Pastor is speaking or increase the speed on our work treadmills and get busier and busier with tasks that don't move us forward and don't risk anything. It's a vicious cycle that puts the onus on us and brings about the temptation of relying only on ourselves. Failure and fear of failure can cause us to retreat into self-reliance, but self-reliance, in the minds of those who desire a relationship with God, begets failure. What is a church leader to do?

We'll talk about that in a later chapter, but it might be helpful now to look at how other segments of society respond to failure.

Failures . . . or Necessary Risks?

In his excellent book *The Power of Habit: Why We Do What We Do in Life and Business,* Charles Duhigg explores how institutions develop good keystone habits. Among other organizations, Duhigg highlights NASA, which has implemented routines that encourages engineers to take more risks. More risks, of course, also mean greater chances for failure. Instead of feeling bad about the failures, though, NASA engineers have now learned to celebrate them. "When unmanned rockets exploded on takeoff, *department heads would applaud*, so that everyone would know their division had tried and failed, but at least they had tried. Eventually, mission control filled with applause every time something expensive blew up. It became an organizational habit" (emphasis mine)[10]

Can you imagine a church or denominational board meeting where people took time to cheer ministry experiments that totally tanked? I can't either. Instead, we wring our hands and become ever more anxious about keeping our religious institutions financially stable. Of course, I'm not advocating poor financial stewardship, but there is a stark difference between how the church (and a lot of society) view failure and how other creative and risk-taking organizations perceive failure. We see some examples in the entrepreneurial world.

A somewhat recent phenomenon among entrepreneurs is the creation of what are called "F***-up Nights." FUNs started in Mexico City in 2012, when a group of friends/entrepreneurs commiserated over drinks, all of them talking about how their start-up businesses were failing. At the end of the evening, they agreed that the conversation had been one of the best they'd ever had, and they hatched the idea of creating what have become anti-TED talks. FUNs are now in more than 120 cities around the world and in fifty different countries. (What's interesting to note is, for now anyway, this seems to be a much more popular thing in other countries. When I looked at a map on the FUN web site to see if I could find one in Chicago, the United States looked pretty bare. Perhaps Americans are still learning how to accept and embrace failure.

The premise of the evening is pretty simple. Wherever the FUN is located—usually a public venue, like a bar—each speaker is given seven minutes and is allowed ten images to share about the f***-up. A question and answer session follows. Each night usually has three to four speakers. That's it. There's laughter, knowing nods, perhaps a few tears and, hopefully, people walk out of there feeling a bit better about their own f***-ups. All of this doesn't come naturally. In an October 2014 article about FUNs in the magazine *Fast Company,* Steffan Bankier, a co-organizer of the New York FUN, said that the word "failure" has a lot of baggage. "I wish there was another word we could use, because learning from a real f***-up is actually very valuable, so it's not really a failure."[11]

There are a lot of reasons why FUNs strike a chord and why they're so popular. It's refreshing to see others be vulnerable, and it's also valuable to see how others respond to failure—hearing someone else give a post-mortem on a failed venture is very helpful, so you can be better prepared if you face a similar situation. It doesn't protect you from stubbing your toe, but, if you truly learn from someone else's failure, it may at least remind you to wear shoes.

Hearing about failures is particularly helpful when these stories come from others who seemingly are succeeding. When we take a risk in ministry and it doesn't go as well as we'd like, knowing that a Hero Pastor has also taken risks and has also fallen on his or her face lets us know that we're not alone. The adage holds true: Misery loves company. So, on behalf of countless church leaders, let me make a request to all the Hero Pastors out there: Tell us how you failed! We've heard about your successes. Wonderful. Congratulations. We now have some helpful guidelines. But to *really* have an impact, share your f***-ups, too.

I don't mean to just call out the Hero Pastors. We all learn from each other when we're vulnerable and admit not everything we try is a rousing success. Not every ministry brings masses of people to Christ. How great would it be at large denominational gatherings if, instead of us seeing videos of groundbreaking churches and inspirational leaders, we see someone stand up and say, "Let me tell about a risk we took this year and how it really blew up in our face." I guarantee you'll have the attention of everyone in the room.

Recovery groups know the power of vulnerability and shared stories of brokenness. The first step in Alcoholics Anonymous is the admission of being powerless over alcohol. Making this admission opens a door and issues an invitation to listeners to enter into the story. A connection is made between the speaker and those gathered. The listener may feel less lonely. *I'm not the only one.* That, in turn, hopefully reminds us that we do not have to depend on ourselves, but on God.

Scripture shows us where this ultimate reliance should be: "Trust in the Lord with all your heart, and do not rely on your own insight. In all your ways acknowledge him, and he will make straight your paths. Do not be wise in your own eyes; fear the Lord, and turn away from evil. It will be a healing for your flesh and a refreshment for your body" (Proverbs 3:5-8). The psalmist says something similar: "Unless the Lord builds the house, those who build it labor in vain. Unless the Lord guards the city, the guard keeps watch in vain. It is in vain that you rise up early and go late to rest, eating the bread of anxious toil; for he gives sleep to his beloved" (Psalm 127:1-2).

Here's the challenge, though. It's not always easy to depend on others, even God. We don't *like* to admit our failures, even if the disclosure puts us in good company. Christians have language for confessing our shortcomings (like repentance), but it still doesn't come easily. We still feel a mixture of shame and vulnerability that is painful. When we muster up the courage to name the misstep, however (like David when he says that Saul's armor doesn't fit), that vulnerability opens up a space for your own growth, and it opens up the possibility of stronger relationships.

I'm a church planter whose parents were both pastors so I've spent my whole life in traditional churches. I loved that planting gave me a chance to think outside of the box and rethink what worship looks like. On our first Christmas Eve service after public launch, I thought it would be fun to tie the theme in with Will Ferrell's movie *Elf* and talk about gifts that the elf brought to the world and compare them to gifts Jesus brings to us. The youth dressed up like elves and handed out symbols of the sermon themes throughout the service ranging from gym socks to purple ornaments. Suffice it to say that Will Ferrell and baby Jesus weren't the perfect combination that I had imagined, and that service has become our litmus test for just how awful a worship service can be. Now I have a worship team that pulls me back to earth when my out-of-the-box ideas go a little too, far.

—Rachel Gilmore
Founding Pastor, The Gathering at Scott Memorial UMC

I learned pretty early in my ministry that when I spoke of my personal foibles and doubts in my sermons, laity responded with relief and appreciation. That honesty helped me take a closer look at my own habits and behaviors so that I could offer those to God and remember that my ministry is not all about me. That honesty also gave others the freedom to do the same and heighten their desire to be engaged in bold ministry with others.

The opportunity to practice vulnerability is another possible reason why FUNs are growing. When we hear someone else say he doesn't have his act together, the burden we may be feeling about our own failures is often lifted, which hopefully will free us to keep trying and risking. Sharing failures helps us learn from each other's mistakes, and it also helps the people talking about the mistakes in the same way confessing our sins helps. Seeing the shortcoming and naming it unburdens us from carrying it around and frees us to learn from it.

Again, from the *Fast Company* article, one of the founders of FUNs, Leticia Grasca, tells of the time when an entrepreneur named Luis Cabrera was talking about one of his f***-ups and he stopped in the middle of the presentation. Grasca remembers him saying, " 'I am sorry, I just realized that I was wrong. I am the f***-up.' In the end," Grasca continued, "he said that [naming his role in the process] had been like an exorcism."

Naming the failure can be freeing, and it can remove the façades we erect that communicate that we have our lives all put together. And knowing we are not alone in our failures moves us to get back up and risk again.

A Marathon Fail

After sitting at the Red Cross tent for a good half-hour, I realized I had two options. I could end my race and get a ride back to the finish line. I could admit that my injury and the lack of training were just too great of hurdles to overcome. That would make sense to many, and it would save me from having to share my race time, which, by the time I was at the tent, was already *a lot* slower than the time I ran to qualify for Boston. Going public with my time would embarrass me. It wouldn't have been *right* to be embarrassed by it; it's just the feelings I was experiencing at the time. The other option would have been to stand up and walk/stagger/ maybe even crawl my way to the finish, and my time would be there for all the world to see.

I chose the latter option.

As I made my way to Boylston Street, which is where the marathon's finish is located, a funny thing happened. No one laughed. No one mocked me. No one cared that I felt like I had failed. Instead, I was one of thousands of other runners receiving cheers and encouragement from the Boston crowd that day. In fact, I received more than generic cheers. Volunteers at the start of the race offered to write a runner's name on their arms with big, black magic markers so that spectators could personalize their encouragement. As I got closer and closer to the end, I heard my name over and over, and it drowned out the self-defeating voices I heard earlier. "Christian! Christian! You're almost there! You've done it! You've finished!"

As I think about that day, those are the voices I continue to hear. They're seared in my memory, like the voices from a great cloud of witnesses. In many ways, I think it's the voice of God bespeaking my belovedness, which is the voice we need to hear over and over.

2

BELOVEDNESS IS
OUR HOME STATION

Teenagers go through all kinds of rites of passage, and our daughter went through one not too long ago. This rite is particular to city-dwelling teens, but it was a momentous occasion nonetheless. Just before she turned fourteen, Caroline rode the subway by herself.

My wife and I had no idea if Caroline was the "right" age. As with most parenting decisions, there's no Grand Manual that tells you when exactly your child is old enough to do any number of things, like going to the park by herself (seven or eight?) or going on a date (thirty-two seems about right). Some parents may think we waited too long, and others probably figure, "You let her do what?" But she seemed mature enough, and the thought of not having to fight traffic on Michigan Avenue to pick her up from school was appealing. So we asked if she was ready, and she took the question in stride and confidently answered yes.

She would only be traveling during the day and, especially for her first ride alone, she wouldn't have to walk very far to get to the train station she needed, but, of course, we had to go through a list of things to be aware of. We made sure she knew how to use the fare-card reader. We quizzed her on which train line to take ("The Red Line"), which trains went north ("The ones going toward Howard") and which ones went south ("To 95th"). The biggest thing we communicated (and we did this over and over again) was which station was her "home" station. Our kids have lived in the city for six years and have ridden the train numerous times, so they should know that "Roosevelt" is the right answer; the stop they get off to go to our home. That didn't stop us from testing Caroline:

> Me: "Which stop do you get off?"
> Caroline: "Roosevelt, Dad."
> Me (two hours later): "Hey, Caroline, which stop is yours?"
> Caroline: "Still Roosevelt."
> Me (one hour later): "Say, by the way—"
> Caroline (with perhaps the slightest eye roll): "Roosevelt."

We were satisfied that she knew this information deep in her core, that she would never forget it, that even if she happened to get on the train going the wrong way, she knew that Roosevelt was where she had to end up. Roosevelt was home. The first ride took place with no incidents, and she made it home safely, much to the relief of her mother and me.

There are certain truths and beliefs that all parents want ingrained in their children's heads, and they will emphasize these things over and over (and over) until their kids know them deeply. Likewise, if you ask most people of faith what is the one thing that

God wants them know—that explicit truth, that core belief—I hope they'd say this: God loves me. Young Christians learn the familiar song at an early age to help them remember this: Jesus loves me, this I know.

Here's the problem, though, that I think many (including church leaders) struggle with. They can *say* that Jesus loves them, and they can communicate this truth to their congregations, but may not truly believe it themselves. Knowing this love, knowing that this love matters more than anything and that this love is the ultimate defining characteristic of you as a child of God is, I believe, the key to rebounding from and persevering through failure. Not knowing that Jesus loves you and not knowing it deeply makes it a lot more tempting to characterize yourself in other ways, including defining yourself by the success or failure of your ministry. But more about that later in this chapter. For now, let's take a look at a couple reasons *why* this message of God's love may not sink in.

Strings Attached

A couple of years ago, our household was asked to be a Nielsen Family. If you've ever had a favorite TV show canceled because its Nielsen ratings were too low, you can blame families like ours. Nielsen has been the industry standard for years in measuring how and what media individuals consume. I don't know how we were selected (I'd like to think it wasn't because we watched more television than your average American family!), but the offer seemed pretty great. I remember the offer saying each individual in the household could make up to $60 a month and all we would have to do is wear a device that was similar to a pager and that device would measure all the media we were taking in. I kept looking for the fine print because, as I saw it, they were paying me the equivalent of a nice meal at a restaurant every month just to watch *House of Cards*. How could this be a bad thing?

As with many offers that seem too good to be true, though, this one followed suit. Instead of $60 a month, it was more like $15, and when they said they wanted us to wear the pager all the time, they weren't kidding. We would get frequent phone calls with gentle reminders if one of us wasn't wearing the pager. Plus, it was more of a pain to wear the thing than I thought it would be, and I'd often wonder, why are we doing this? Is it worth it?

This is a small and fairly trite example of an incident where there were strings attached to something that seemed too be good to be true, but over the years at Urban Village, we often talk to individuals who have experienced a "strings attached" philosophy with their faith lives. This is particularly true for our LGTBQ members, several of whom attended a church as they grew up that preached about the power of God's love . . . unless you're gay. They want to believe in God's love, but they've heard there are really big conditions to receiving that love so they either leave the church, or it takes them a while to really accept that God's love is unconditional.

When I think about leaders in the mainline church, my first thought is that surely they know differently. Having a "strings attached" philosophy to God's love isn't something they struggle with, is it? Perhaps not consciously, but I wonder how many internal conversations leaders have that tie God's love to performing well in their jobs, or living a sterling personal life, or having a steadfast faith that buoys them in the midst of life's storms.

I don't experience many leaders promoting God's conditional love, but I have to wonder if they struggle to accept their belovedness as the key part of their identity—if their identity is still tied up in how "good" of a Christian leader they are.

Keep It Simple? That's Stupid

Another reason why some church leaders may not deeply internalize "Jesus loves me, this I know" is that they feel like it's time to move onto more sophisticated theology. It is a child's song, after all. They may subconsciously recall Paul's statement in 1 Corinthians 13:11 ("When I was a child, I spoke like a child, I thought like a child, I reasoned like a child; when I became an adult, I put an end to childish ways.") and believe that, "God loves me," is too simple to meditate upon. Better to wrestle with theological giants and reflect on deep epistemological questions than to waste time with "Jesus loves me."

That's why the oft-told story of Karl Barth is worth repeating again. In a 2013 blog post on the Patheos web site, Roger Olson, Foy Valentine Professor of Christian Theology of Ethics at George W. Truett Theological Seminary of Baylor University, summarized the story: Barth was at Rockefeller Chapel at the University of Chicago in 1962, and, after his lecture, a questioner asked Barth if he could summarize his life's work in theology in a single sentence.[1] Barth allegedly said, "Yes, I can. In the words of a song I learned at my mother's knee, 'Jesus loves me, this I know, for the Bible tells me so.'" Olson was using this post as an attempt to find out if, indeed, Barth said those things, and he had enough confirmations from eyewitnesses (both at the University of Chicago and at a lecture Barth gave in Richmond, Virginia, where he said something similar) to posit that Barth, indeed, made that statement.

I'm certainly not opposed to robust theological conversations, but I think we set ourselves up for potential faith crises if we believe that we are too sophisticated and well read for the seeming simplicity of God's love for us.

35

One Sunday morning when I was in my early thirties, maybe a decade after I had started preaching, my sermon completely bombed. I don't mean that it simply fell flat; I mean that it completely fell apart. More to the point, I completely fell apart—in front of a large gathering of the new church I'd recently planted.

This failure happened at the beginning of a season when I was intentionally trying to preach from a more emotionally rooted place and with a more conversational style. Pretty close to the beginning of the sermon, I lost my place, I lost my point, and I felt like I was losing my dignity. With every attempt to regain my balance, I slipped farther into a hole that I just couldn't dig out of, no matter how desperately I tried. After five minutes of stumbling, I apologized to the congregation and simply sat down, my face hot with shame and humiliation.

In previous tellings, I've blamed this failure on my laudable attempt to move from my long-term practice of preaching with a manuscript to a new practice of preaching without notes. But if I'm honest, I can't chalk up this experience simply to the risk of trying something new, the fumblings that are a necessary part of learning a new leadership technique.

It was more than that. It was, I have come to believe, one of the many tremors in a seismic shift that God was (and is) instigating to show me the end of the shallow reserves of my false self, to crumble the idol of ministry based on personality, to trip me toward an existential hitting-bottom. When I told my spiritual director about it later in the week, she said, quite unbelievably, "It's probably good that it happened."

Here's to the terrible gift of God's seismic activity.

—Trey Hall
Co-Founder of Urban Village Church
Ministry Coach with the Epicenter Group

It's Not New

A third reason why church leaders may forget their belovedness is that this news is, well, not new. We've heard it countless times, preached it even more, and so the repetitiveness of this message in our minds contributes to the power of this truth.

I find it interesting to watch how airplane passengers respond when flight attendants give the instructions about what to do in case of emergency. You would think that everyone would be paying close attention to these instructions because, well, *the plane could crash.* Why *wouldn't* you want to know every single detail of what to do if the plane goes down? Yes, please, Ms. Flight Attendant, tell and show me again how my seat cushion can be used as a flotation device! Of course, the attendants should be doing their very best to have the passengers hear and learn this information because it is potentially life-saving. Occasionally, though, and perhaps not surprisingly, the attendants have weary and bored looks on their faces. You can't really blame them because they've held the seat belts over their heads to show you how to fasten them thousands of times *and* they have a less-than-captivated audience. Every time they direct people to where the exit rows are and every time they've gone through the laminated safety card in the seat pocket in front of you, what do they see when they look out at the passengers? Nothing. Or, more accurately, the tops of peoples' heads. Business executives are looking down at their phones and vacationers are already sleeping or staring off into space. For the most part, the passengers are doing this because they've heard this life-saving news time and again, so why listen again?

For some (many?) people of faith, they react the same way when they hear the life-saving and life-changing news that God loves them. I've heard it before, they would say, so I'm just going to go back to watching cat videos on my phone. I learned all that as a child—wake me when something *new* comes along.

This third reason—that the truth of God's love is old news—is probably the one I struggle with the most. The truth that God loves me and loves me deeply was something that hadn't penetrated my life as much as I thought it had. I was one of those airline passengers, having heard the same spiel so many times that it lost its impact.

It's Too Sentimental

Right up there with the mistaken belief that God's love is old news, another reason why I hadn't embraced my belovedness (and perhaps others don't) is occasional discomfort with sentimentality. For example, comments like these from Henri Nouwen's book *Life of the Beloved* used to make me squirm: "When I know that I am chosen, I know that I have been seen as a special person. Someone has noticed me in my uniqueness and has expressed a desire to know me, to come closer to me, to love me."[2] Or this: "We need an ongoing blessing that allows us to hear in an ever-new way that we belong to a loving God who will never leave us alone, but will remind us always that we are guided by love on every step of our lives."[3]

Nouwen is describing how God "takes" or "chooses" us, and when I read a statement like this, I roll my eyes a bit and think of "caring nurturer but not a licensed therapist" Stuart Smalley on *Saturday Night Live* ("I'm good enough. I'm smart enough. And doggone it, people like me.") or any other self-help guru. Sure, I'd think, I am loved, but I don't need to *dwell* on that. What about sin? Sin needs at least equal (if not more) time. What about the need to go out and *do* something? I can't just sit around wallowing in God's love, can I? Actually, yes, I can. And should.

Reclaiming Belovedness

My dog Winnie loves to go out on our back porch (and, because we're city-dwellers, I use the term "porch" rather loosely; it's more of a balcony right off of our kitchen) and lie in the sun. She is a picture of contentment as she rests there and soaks in the warmth. She's not worrying if she's checking off her Dog To-Do List or whether she's giving equal lounge time to other parts of our townhome. She loves the sun and will bask in it. In the past, I've rarely allowed myself to just sit and bask in God's love. Instead, I would pause in God's love. Pay it a quick visit before dashing off to other theological or missional "balconies." Because of my inability to bask and really listen about the news of God's love, when challenges came up in the life of Urban Village, I sometimes wasn't able to handle it very well.

The most difficult challenge happened the summer of 2014. I'll say more in Chapter 5 about the specifics of why I went through a real vocational and spiritual crisis, but, for now I'll summarize by saying that the site I was overseeing had moved locations and was experiencing decreasing worship attendance.

At the same time, some of Urban Village's other sites were flourishing and, instead of my fully celebrating this good news, because my whole sense of self had become dependent not on my belovedness but on the acclaim the success of *my* site, I became a little bitter (sometimes more than a little) and started drowning in self-pity and declining self-worth. My despondency got to the point where, during a breakfast meeting with my ministry partner and UVC's other lead pastor Trey Hall, I told him that I was seriously considering leaving to do something else, that maybe someone else could/should take my place and turn things around. Trey, as he always does, offered a sympathetic ear. Although he didn't agree with my assessment that it was all my fault, he promised to be with me in my discernment.

Throughout my ministry, a place that's been truly holy ground and has helped center me is St. Procopius Abbey, a Benedictine monastery in Chicago's western suburbs. I'd been going to St. Procopius for more than twenty years, and the peace of the grounds and the hospitality offered me by the monks never failed to restore my soul. I needed some major restoration.

One of my former spiritual directors had recommended St. Procopius to me in the early 1990s, and he suggested that, at least for the first visit, I should take no books, but simply pray, sleep, and eat. I've never been able to follow that suggestion (the taking-no-books suggestion, that is—I gladly sleep and eat and, yes, pray), though, and on this particular trip, two of the books I brought along were the aforementioned *Life of the Beloved* by Henri Nouwen and *Abba's Child* by Brennan Manning. These would prove to be inspired (and inspiring) choices.

As with many of my friends and peers, Nouwen has been a spiritual hero of mine, but I'd never read Manning before. I'd heard a lot about him, but never took the time to sit down with one of his books. Pretty quickly, though, his insights into humanity cut me to the core. One of the early chapters of *Abba's Child* is called "The Imposter." Manning uses the character Leonard Zelig from the Woody Allen movie *Zelig* as his prototype for a human imposter. Manning describes Zelig as a "celebrity nonentity who fits in everywhere because he actually changes his personality to each evolving situation."[4] Manning confessed that he saw himself as Zelig, one who was a radical poseur who wears many different masks because he fears rejection from others. Impostors, Manning notes, are preoccupied with acceptance and approval. Manning nailed it for me. I, too, was preoccupied with acceptance and approval. Receiving acclaim was a pillar of my faith. Jesus shares a parable in Matthew 7:24-27 that goes like this:

> Everyone then who hears these words of mine and acts on them will be like a wise man who built his house on rock. The rain fell, the floods came, and the winds blew and beat on that house, but it did not fall, because it had been founded on rock. And everyone who hears these words of mine and does not act on them will be like a foolish man who built his house on sand. The rain fell, and the floods came, and the winds blew and beat against that house, and it fell—and great was its fall!

So in case you're missing the connection here: Me building my sense of self on acclaim = Foolish man building his house on sand.

Paul Graham is a British essayist and software programmer. A few years ago, someone pointed me to an excellent online article he wrote called, "How to Do What You Love." He reflects on the dangers of seeking prestige, a close cousin of acclaim. He first offers this advice on what one should *not* do in order to do what you love:

> What you should not do, I think, is worry about the opinion of anyone beyond your friends. You shouldn't worry about prestige. Prestige is the opinion of the rest of the world. . . . Prestige is like a powerful magnet that warps even your beliefs about what you enjoy.[5]

Or how about this, a more faith-based reflection on prestige and notoriety from Thomas à Kempis, who wrote a fifteenth-century book (his pithy style and structure reminds me of a

Renaissance blog!) called *The Imitation of Christ*: "Many in this world care little for the service of God and their lives end up in futility. They perish through their own ambition, because they chose to be famous rather than humble. The truly great are humble in mind, and consider public acclamations to be worthless."[6]

I had fallen into a trap where I was doing everything Graham advised not to do and what à Kempis warned against. I *did* worry about the opinion of imaginary critics and observers. I felt I *was* perishing through my own ambition. In turn, this warped my beliefs about what I enjoyed and, I would add, what I loved. More seriously, it warped my sense of Who loved me.

In *Abba's Child*, Manning states clearly what *should* be giving us our identity and sense of self: "While the impostor draws his identity from past achievements and the adulation of others the true self claims identity in its belovedness."[7]

That, friends, is sacred truth and (at least for me) is hard as hell to live into. The gap between drawing worth from achievements and adulation to drawing worth from being beloved of God was unbelievably wide for me, and I wasn't quite sure how to close it. I was tempted to try to make up that gap all by myself, but, thankfully, I'd had enough experience in being in faithful relationships with others to know that I couldn't do it up alone.

Every other year, my wife Anne and I spend Thanksgiving with her aunt and uncle in Fort Wayne, Indiana. It's always a large gathering of family, and one of the highlights is heading out to their back acreage to help Anne's Uncle Will build a big bonfire while also exploring the woods. There's a creek that runs just to the east of their property, which is always a popular place for younger members of the family to play. If the water is not too high, an islet appears in the middle of the creek, and one year I went back with my kids to check things out. Some of my nieces and nephews were already on this islet, exploring and having fun.

My kids, of course, wanted to join them, but the only way to get there was to cross the creek on a fallen tree that stretched from the bank to the islet. On the one hand, this didn't seem like a big deal. The tree was fairly wide and the creek couldn't have been more than two feet deep. My kids were younger, though, and I could tell they weren't sure what to do because the islet seemed so far away and the tree *seemed* awfully narrow. They wanted to play with their cousins on what seemed like the Island of Adventure, but the gap between where they were (having a mildly good time with Dad) and where their cousins were (who clearly were having the best time ever) seemed enormous and daunting. They finally decided that they wanted to cross the gap, but they had their own unique ways of making the trek. Caroline was going to get there not by walking across the tree, but by kneeling down, hugging the tree and then inching her way across like a caterpillar. It took a while, but she made it. My son Ethan also wanted to cross, but his strategy was for me to hold his hand as we walked along the fallen tree together. I thought that was a great idea because I wasn't 100 percent confident that I'd make it across without getting wet myself. He held on tightly and we carefully made it to the islet. They both crossed that gap, but they both really needed someone or something to hold tightly onto.

My own spiritual gap between desiring prestige and acclaim and living into my belovedness seemed just as wide and daunting. I knew I wanted to cross into belovedness, but I knew I couldn't make it alone. My time on that retreat at the abbey was like God offering a hand for me to hold onto, and I slowly inched my way across. I started to bask in belovedness.

After I read *Abba's Child* and started in on Nouwen's book, belovedness clearly became the theme of my retreat. I no longer was rolling my eyes at this supposed new-age thinking. I yearned to believe that I was beloved. I thirsted for it, like the invitation from the prophet Isaiah to come to the living waters ("All of you who are thirsty, come to the water!"). It finally dawned on me that being beloved is the foundation of my faith; this would never change no matter how effective my ministry was, no matter what the worship numbers looked like, and no matter how much I failed (or seemed to fail). I was beloved.

Manning encourages his readers: "Define yourself radically as one beloved by God. God's love for you and his choice of you constitute your worth. Accept that, and let it become the most important thing in your life."[8] Nouwen echoes these sentiments: "From the moment we claim the truth of being the Beloved, we are faced with the call to become who we are. . . . Becoming the Beloved means letting the truth of our Belovedness become enfleshed in everything we think, say, or do."[9]

So many of those early faith lessons came crashing down on me. Something I'd heard all my life, starting when I accepted Christ as a child and including the countless times I'd preached this as a pastor, was actually sinking in and becoming *true*. What a joy it is when the things you say to others actually become the things you feel in your heart and believe. I don't think I'm the only one who has struggled with this spiritual inconsistency. Some giants of the faith have faced this same challenge.

Urban Village is a United Methodist Church and I am a United Methodist pastor. I know in our post-denominational age, labels like Methodist or Presbyterian or Episcopalian don't mean much (and seem about as relevant as eight-track tape players), but I've been a lifelong United Methodist, in part because of the church's founders, John and Charles Wesley, and their vision for holistic faith and ministry. In his book, *Recapturing the Wesley's Vision*, Paul Wesley Chilcote spells out the ways in which the Wesleys had a "both/and" kind of faith. They brought together faith *and* works, the head *and* the heart, Christ *and* culture, piety *and* mercy.

John Wesley was an eighteenth-century priest in the Church of England, who created a movement within the church that became known as Methodism. (There's some disagreement as to why it was called this, but the general thinking is that it was because its members were so methodical about their spiritual practices.) Wesley went to Oxford University as a young man, became a priest, and was fascinated by and intensely determined to make his Christianity *real*. He could recite biblical truths with the best of them. He spent hours in prayer and meticulously measured his acts of piety. But he struggled to feel the assurance of his faith, which made him wonder whether he really was a Christian.

Wesley went to Georgia (then an American colony) as a missionary in 1735 and stayed for three tumultuous years. He went to preach the gospel to Native Americans, but he struggled with live the gospel himself. In a letter he wrote to a resident in Georgia, Wesley noted, "My chief motive, to which all the rest are subordinate, is the hope of saving my own soul. I hope to learn the true sense of the gospel of Christ by preaching it to the heathen."[10] A month after he returned from Georgia in January 1738, he wrote this in his journal: "I went to America, to convert the Indians; but oh! who shall convert me? who, what is He that will deliver me from this evil heart of mischief? I have a fair summer religion."[11] Here was a man who struggled with knowing deeply the truths that he was espousing.

Not long after returning, Wesley had his famous conversion to felt faith on May 24, 1738, when he felt his heart being "strangely warm'd." While I, too, have drawn inspiration from this first-hand account, I'm drawn to what Wesley says right after the "strangely warm'd" comment: "I felt I did trust in Christ, Christ alone for salvation, and an assurance was given me that he had taken away my sins, even mine, and saved me from the law of sin and death."[12] *Even mine.* It's those two words that have a big impact on me.

The truth of God's love and forgiveness became real for Wesley in that moment. He knew it was true for others *and* it was true for him. I could relate. I don't want to say that God's love had never been real for me because it had, but I rediscovered it in a way that made it feel personal. I had been telling others that they were beloved, and I knew that they were. It was sinking in that I was (and am) beloved, too. Even me.

The numerous Scripture passages that proclaim God's love for us became clear again to me, especially one particular biblical story having to do with the beginning of Jesus' ministry and life.

Jesus Gets the Message

When we think about beginnings and Jesus, many people understandably reflect on the story of his birth. A few may go to the book of John and its proclamation that in the beginning was the Word and the Word was God and the Word was with God. These are all great places to start, but I've always been drawn to the beginning of Jesus' adulthood and public ministry as told by Matthew, Mark, and Luke. I'm specifically speaking of his baptism. (The book of John also touches on it, but it's not quite as explicit as the other three).

Immediately after Jesus is baptized (Matthew 3; Luke 3; Mark 1), Jesus emerges from the water and, according to Matthew, a voice from the heavens declares: "This is my Son, the Beloved, with whom I am well pleased" (Matthew 3:17; Luke and Mark's versions make Jesus' emergence from the waters more personal as the heavenly voice tells Jesus directly: "*You* are my Son, the Beloved; with you I am well pleased" [Luke 3:22; Mark 1:11, emphasis mine]). This is the money quote, the verse to memorize and stick on your refrigerator so that it's always before you. But Jesus does a couple things before this revelation that should catch our attention.

John (Jesus' cousin and the one who will be doing the baptizing) is introduced in these books with the description of his take-no-prisoners persona and minimalist lifestyle. Jesus then enters the scene. In Matthew's version, Jesus' intentions are clear: He wants to be baptized and receive this blessing. I don't know if he was expecting a heavenly voice that would affirm his belovedness, but I think we should pay attention to his intentionality:

> At that time Jesus came from Galilee to the Jordan River so that John would baptize him. John tried to stop him and said, "I need to be baptized by you, yet you come to me?" Jesus answered, "Allow me to be baptized now. This is necessary to fulfill all righteousness."
>
> Matt. 3:13-15, CEB

Something (or Someone) compelled Jesus to approach John and go through this experience, knowing that he would need this not only to fulfill all righteousness (as he declares) but also to sustain him during his ministry. He knew the need for it and intentionally placed himself in a position to receive it. Jesus also shows vulnerability here. He acknowledges his need for this heavenly blessing and affirmation, and he often reminds his followers of his inability to do anything without God's presence and power. Jesus' awareness of his dependence on God is especially true in the gospel of John ("Jesus said to them, 'Very truly, I tell you, the Son can do nothing on his own, but only what he sees the Father doing; for whatever the Father does, the Son does likewise'" [John 5:19]). The text in Matthew doesn't tell us if Jesus senses he is losing face or respect. I don't know if that matters to him. I do know he finds this baptism necessary.

Jesus gives us a wonderful model of intentionality and vulnerability here. Time and again, Jesus leaves behind large crowds, the sick and lonely, and goes away to pray and be reminded of who he is and how much he is loved. Maybe he also needs this reminder because his life is not filled with constant accolades and successes.

One of my favorite biblical transitions happens right after the baptism/blessing: Jesus is immediately driven into the wilderness (Matthew 4:1-11; Luke 4:1-13) to be tested and tempted by Satan. There is no reception after his baptism, complete with a nice sheet cake and mixed nuts. Jesus faces one of his biggest challenges right away. I'd like to think that in the midst of the temptations placed before him, Jesus kept hearing that voice, maybe even whispering it to himself: "You are my beloved. With you I am well pleased." I especially like the way that the Common English Bible translates this verse: "You are my Son, whom I dearly love; in you I find happiness" (Luke 3:22, CEB). If you knew this truth deep in your core, if you used it as a kind of mantra in your daily life, don't you think it would help in your day-to-day life? Especially when you find yourself up against challenges and failing at big and small tasks?

One of the most powerful scenes in the movie, *Good Will Hunting,* comes when Will and his therapist, Sean, begin talking about the contents of a folder that entails all of the abuses Will experienced as a child. Sean says, "I don't know a lot, but you see this?" He holds up the folder. "It's not your fault." Sean then begins a mantra that he repeats nine more times: "It's not your fault."

At first, Will keeps saying that he knows it's not his fault, but Sean says, no, he doesn't really know it. Not yet. Which is why Sean keeps repeating over and over that it's not his fault. After the tenth time, Will breaks down and begins weeping in Sean's arms.

When we experience the pain of failure, whether it's leading a committee that is unproductive or starting a new ministry that doesn't get going, we need to hear over and over the words that Jesus hears: You are my child, whom I dearly love; in you I find

Megan was smart, beautiful, and charismatic, a natural leader in our campus ministry. The first day we met, she challenged me: "You're either the most real person I've ever met or the biggest fake." Uncertain how to respond, I told her she should hang around and find out.

She did.

Over the next two years, Megan's story of sexual abuse unfolded. One night after a worship service I found her in fetal position in my office. The university counseling center recommended psychotherapy, so I called a therapist friend for a referral. I gave Megan the doctor's name, and she began treatment.

Weeks later I returned to grad school, and Megan vanished. At Christmas I called her. Megan said that the therapist I recommended had sexually abused her, so she ran. That was the last time we spoke.

My stomach lurched. I had placed a student I loved, a student who desperately needed help, into the care of a predator. Lord, have mercy. Amen.

—Kenda Creasy Dean
Mary D. Synnott Professor of Youth, Church and Culture
at Princeton Theological Seminary
Author, *Almost Christian: What the Faith of Our Teenagers
Is Telling the American Church*

happiness. Here's the good news: What God said to Jesus that day, God says to you every day. *You are my child, whom I dearly love; in you I find happiness.* This news may seem banal or even benign, but we need to hear it over and over and over again until it finally sinks in. This is the foundation of our faith, friends. I cannot emphasize enough. Now, you might say to yourself, Yes, yes, I've heard this. I believe this. How can this be the secret to responding to failure?

I'll point you back to my example about pre-flight instructions on an airplane. The attendants are giving life-saving information, and yet the good majority of passengers have heard it before. It's nothing new. The news about belovedness may not be new *per se*, but it is life-saving. The news of your belovedness is good and life-saving; news that you must hear and be reminded of. It is so hard to come back from and receive the benefits of failure without hearing *You are my child, whom I dearly love; in you I find happiness* over and over again until it becomes as natural as breathing.

Intentional Messaging

Remembering that we are beloved takes intentionality, daily putting ourselves in God's presence so that we can receive this powerful message that is for us, just as it was for Jesus. When we take this truth for granted, we allow other truths (e.g. that you're a failure) to worm their way into our hearts and to take the place of the core truth of our belovedness. My first prayer every morning is that throughout the day, I will put myself in a position to hear, "You are my child, whom I dearly love; in you I find happiness." I say this as soon as I wake up. This foundation should become routine for all of us, for the person new to faith and for those who have followed Christ their whole lives.

I was fortunate that all four of my grandparents lived until I was well into my adulthood. Having a relationship with all of them formed me in significant ways, not only because I had a chance to hear them tell and watch them live their stories, but also because they gave me a cache of memories I treasure. For a few summers when I was a tween and young teen, I would stay for a week with my cousin at my Grandma and Grandpa Coon's home. I have many wonderful memories from those July weeks, and nearly all of them involve small snippets of daily life including meals shared, wisdom offered, and routines observed. One of those routines was the way my grandparents said good-bye to each other every morning.

My grandmother would always prepare a tasty breakfast, and so it was worth getting up early to enjoy that meal with her and my grandfather. As he got up from the table and collected his things to go to work, my grandmother also left the table and walked him to the door. As I ate my eggs and toast, I could hear them whispering to each other for a few minutes, though I couldn't always make out what they were saying. I sensed that they were talking about the day ahead, but whatever the topic of conversation, these whispers would be interrupted by quick kisses. *Whisper, whisper, kiss.* Grandpa would then leave for the day and Grandma would come back to the kitchen table. The next morning, same routine. Fix breakfast, eat with us, and then head to the doorway for a few minutes. *Whisper, kiss, whisper, whisper, kiss.*

I doubt that these kisses were always filled with great romantic passion, and the conversation probably often included the "boring" stuff of our everyday lives, but when my grandmother died in the summer of 2015, they had been married seventy years. One of the many reasons for the strength and length of their union, I think, was because they sensed how important it was to communicate their love to each other and so they made it part of their regular routine. Every day they would whisper these sentiments as quiet reminders to each other about the foundational truth of their relationship.

One of the challenges for many of those who have been faithful to their relationship with God for many years is that they think there should necessarily be something groundbreaking in that relationship—maybe a new facet of God's personality to explore or an aspect of theology to learn. There is truth in this. We should explore the mystery of that relationship, and we will always learn new things about God's character. But that does not preclude going back to the basics. Indeed, it *can't* preclude it. God's love for us must always be the first and last thing we know. There are times, though, as there were (and are) for me, when I stray from those basics. This allows fear and anxiety to take hold, which exacerbates my sense of failure. That's why we need the "boring-ness" of routine. We cannot take our belovedness for granted because this truth is more powerful than we realize.

Who You Really Are

Social media certainly has affected how we see ourselves. My Facebook feed sometimes features the latest results of some online personality quiz that a friend took. These quizzes are usually found on a website like Buzzfeed, and they let you know what state you should be living in or, according to a quiz I took the other day, which American president you are. (After asking me to choose things like a particular dog from a list of nine options, I learned that apparently I'm Thomas Jefferson.) They're fun exercises, and I suspect they're popular because people are always eager for a slightly humorous look into their true selves. ("Among all the Harry Potter characters, am I really Hermione Granger? What does that say about me?") We try so hard to get a glimpse into who we are because in our culture, we are constantly asked to define (and redefine) ourselves. We feel that pressure when we attend something as innocuous as a dinner party with people you haven't met yet ("So, what do you do for a living? Where do you live? Where are you from? What do you think about this presidential election?"), and we certainly feel it when we engage in social media, making sure our photos and comments tell the world that we have it altogether.

Your true identity is your belovedness, something that isn't terribly exciting to tweet and is something that's easy to forget. Among the many other things that make you truly you, your identity starts with that truth and once you're reminded of that and begin to let it touch on all other aspects of your life (especially your failures), it has a powerful effect. So whatever helpful tool you can utilize that reminds you of your belovedness—a sticky note at your desk, a friend who will check in with you, a breath prayer, a song that you play while you're in the shower—make full use of that tool. It doesn't matter if it seems silly or feels like a crutch. *Use it.*

One of the main questions we get asked about Urban Village's origins is one that the questioner doesn't quite know how to formulate. Essentially it comes down to one word: How? As in, how exactly do you start a church and get people to actually commit to this nebulous thing that doesn't have a building? It's a great question that takes some time to answer, but building relationships is a key component to starting a new (or, really any) faith community. During that first summer of getting this new venture going, Trey and I had the goal of making twenty-five contacts with individuals or groups a week. Those could be meeting someone over coffee or speaking in front of a group or chatting with another parent at a park.

For me, one thing I took advantage of was my membership in a fraternity (for which I also worked for two-and-a-half years). I was able to secure an impressive list of email addresses of fraternity members who lived in Chicago and, instead of cold calling, did "cold messaging." I started each message by telling the recipient that he didn't know me, but that we were part of the same fraternity. I said that I had just moved into the city after years of living in the suburbs because I was starting a new church, and I wanted to meet other city dwellers to get their insights of Chicago living. I assured them that I wasn't going to sell them on the church, but that I simply wanted to hear their Chicago story. (Of course, if they *wanted* to know more about the church, I certainly would tell them.)

As you might imagine, I had a pretty high failure rate, but I was surprised that about 10 to 15 percent of those emails turned into meetings, and I did learn a lot about life in Chicago (albeit from an college-educated male's perspective). One meeting took place in the location where Trey and I had that very first gathering that I described in the Introduction—the Barnes & Noble bookstore. I was to meet a recent Northwestern graduate whose name was Phoenician. We were going to connect in the Starbucks inside the bookstore, but when we arrived, every table was full. We looked for an alternative place to sit down and talk, and we meandered our way through the bookcases and found two chairs in a quiet nook in the fiction section. Phoenician told me his story about growing up in Chicago as the child of Chinese immigrants and said he was interested in this new church we were starting because he had grown up in a church, but he hadn't made much of a connection to one in recent few years.

For someone to express more than a passing interest in the church during one of these meetings I had with fraternity members was a little unusual. They were all nice about it, but the meetings usually went just like I had said it would in the email. The person would tell me about his career, the particular neighborhood he lived in, what he liked (or didn't like) about it, what he saw for his future in the city. A person may have asked a couple questions about the church and me, but the conversation didn't get much further than that. Phoenician, though, kept asking questions, and I wasn't as prepared as I should have been. I haltingly told him why we were doing what we were doing, what we believed, and what was going to make this church different. Here was my chance to make the case for faith and my church, and I felt like I was doing a pretty poor job. I don't remember what I said about God loving all of us, but I certainly don't think I said it very eloquently.

As I finished talking, though, I looked up and noticed that Phoenician's eyes were red and tears were beginning to trickle down his face. I was totally taken aback by this reaction and certainly wasn't expecting it. But his response reminded me of the power of this spiritual truth of God's love that we frequently hear and yet often take for granted. Phoenician needed someone to remind him that God actually loves him. Once that became real again for him, it literally made a world of difference. Phoenician recommitted to his faith life, became one of the first members of our church, and he used his skills to create Urban Village's database!

After I wrote up the story above and sent it to Phoenician to have him look it over to make sure my memory of our first meeting was accurate, he sent me a thoughtful email that included these reflections: "Your words that day [about God's presence and my belovedness] have stayed with me. These were words that were overflowing with kindness, love, and full of grace. They had been the words for which I had been searching for long and far, although I did not know what I had been looking for until then. These words of yours have since been a central pillar and precept of my life."[13]

Phoenician's words were yet another reminder that we must intentionally be reminded of our belovedness every single day, so we don't let anything else define us, because there are plenty of things in our world that will try to do that for us.

So What?

I mentioned in the Introduction my issue with attending the kind of church-growth conference where the speaker implies that if you just write down what he or she is saying (or buy their book or DVD set), then your church will blossom, as if there's merely a mechanical problem and all that's needed is a manual or YouTube video. Responding to failure is more than just a knowing how to fix a broken switch. It goes deeper than that.

My wife and I were re-watching *The King's Speech* the other night. (We happened to be in London at the time and I think there must be some British law that a Colin Firth movie must be playing on some television station at all times.) The movie is a biopic about King George VI and his relationship with a speech therapist named Lionel Logue. The king had a speech impediment and tried all manner of things and saw all manner of experts to fix the problem. There's a heart-wrenching scene in the movie where he (before he was king) practices a speech in front of a microphone. He, of course, can't make it through and stutters even more as he tries harder. His father, King George V, is exasperated. "Just focus! Take your time!" he harshly counsels his son. While George VI did have mechanical speech issues he could work on, Logue also sensed there were deeper emotional issues there, as well, and, tried to get at those as their relationship deepened.

It's tempting to want a few quick fixes to respond to the challenge of failure, and I wish I could point you to a two-minute "how-to" video on YouTube. That's what the future king and his wife wanted. Quick fixes. A few exercises and they'd be on their way. But perhaps they knew there was more to it than that. The same is true for you and me.

Later in the book, I'll reflect on ways we can respond to failure (and also highlight some of the gifts that can come from failure), but before we can tackle the "how-to's" of this process, we must make sure we truly believe and receive the deep and foundational spiritual truth: You are beloved by God. God delights in you. God relishes spending time with you. Once this truth begins to seep into your soul and you daily celebrate and acknowledge it, you can try all manner of things in ministry and life and even screw up royally, knowing that, no matter what, you come back to the One who will receive you with joy and grace. You might say that your home station is Belovedness. And God will do anything to make sure you don't forget that.

3

THE BIBLE TELLS ME SO: SCRIPTURAL STORIES OF FAILURE

One of my favorite chapters from Kathleen Norris' book *Amazing Grace* is simply entitled "Bible." The chapter is only four paragraphs long, but it offers one of the best stories I've ever read about the Scriptures. Norris describes one night when she and her husband were visiting with what she calls "an old-timer, a tough, self-made man in the classic American sense"[1] in a local steakhouse. The man (Norris calls him Arlo) was more talkative than normal and was sharing a story about his grandfather, who was deeply religious. His grandfather gave Arlo and his wife a Bible as a wedding present, "bound in white leather with their names and the date of their wedding set in gold lettering on the cover."[2] Arlo wasn't much of a religious man himself, so they stored it away. His grandfather kept asking him, however, how he liked the Bible he had given them. Arlo was puzzled by this, because his wife had sent him a thank-you note and he'd thanked him in person, but his grandfather kept pestering him about it. Months later, Arlo finally got the Bible out to see what the big deal was, and he discovered his grandfather had put a $20 bill in the front of every book, both Old Testament and New. It was quite a gift—more than $1,300— which, Arlo noted, "was a lot of money in them days."[3]

This is a great story about the discovery of unexpected treasures in the Bible. The Bible has been used for many things throughout its history, including inspiration, guidance, comfort, and, in recent years, a how-to guide for church growth and revitalization. It certainly has been misused as well, as an impetus for violence, unjust condemnation, and racism. As I was thinking about writing a book, though, it struck me that the Bible is also a treasure trove of failure stories. For Christians, of course, our iconic symbol was once seen as the ultimate failure. The cross was used as an execution tool by the Roman Empire to make known its own dominance and emphasize defeat for anyone who suffered this kind of punishment and death. Indeed, Paul notes in 1 Corinthians 1:18 that the message of the cross seems to be folly in the eyes of the world. Followers of the one who suffered this "failure," though, know the power of this symbol. "The cross is a paradoxical religious symbol because it *inverts* the world's value system with the news that hope comes by way of defeat, that suffering an death do not have the last word, that the last shall be first and the first last."[4] Jesus' crucifixion is not the only narrative that flips failure on its head. From the third chapter of Genesis with Adam and Eve's decision to eat the fruit and continuing through the third chapter of Revelation with its list of churches that are churches in name only, there are plenty of examples of faithful women and men who have strayed from God's hopes and desires for them.

These stories are more than helpful reminders that illustrate that we're not alone in messing up our faith lives (though they can do that). The examples also offer insights into how God responds to failure and how failures can deepen our faith lives and strengthen our resolve to continue taking chances in our ministries.

I thought about doing a grand sweep of the Bible and showing representative examples of failure in the Old and New Testaments, but, as is often the case in my own ministry, I was drawn to the gospels and found many rich examples in them. We start off, in fact, with a story that could conceivably be seen as one of Jesus' failures.

Jesus Cleanses Ten Lepers (Luke 17:11-19)

I don't think it's a coincidence that I've become a fan of the New York Times crossword puzzle during my time as a church planter. Starting a new church is filled with mystery and uncertainty (let alone a multi-site new church), so it's a blessed relief to see the puzzle's little boxes laid out in front of me in black and white. There is rarely gray in answering a puzzle (other than the rare occasion when a puzzle creator tries to get cute with his or her puzzle construction), and I always have a small feeling of triumph when I complete one. Certainty. Concreteness. It's nice to have that in my life, because trying to predict when a person might (a) be interested in a relationship with Jesus and (b) be interested in exploring that relationship with your community of faith is anything but certain or concrete.

One of the biggest frustrations in church planting in my particular context is, to put it mildly, the fickleness of humans. ("All people are grass," has become one of my favorite verses from the psalms.) This scenario happens quite often:

A person finds out about Urban Village. Let's call her Eva. Eva attends one of our worship services, and something about the experience moves her deeply. She fills out one of our tear-off slips and includes all the vital information we crave. Name. Street address. Email address. Cell phone. Birthday. On the back of the slip, she checks off almost all the boxes of things she's interested in. Small groups? Check! Membership? Check! Service and justice work? Check! Learning more about financial giving? Check!

Planters crave these responses. At Urban Village, we place a high priority on building relationships, so one of our pastors will usually follow up with someone like Eva to see if she'd like to meet up for coffee. She's pleasantly surprised that a *pastor* would reach out to her like this, and she readily agrees. We meet at a coffee shop, and she shares her story, and she also talks about how much she loved the worship. She's never experienced anything like this before. She's had either bad or boring experiences of church in the past, but Urban Village is different, she exudes. The pastor (let's be honest, it's me) eats this up and looks for ways to get Eva engaged.

Eva starts attending regularly and may even write an email saying what a difference Urban Village has made in her life. She gives a shout out to the church on her Facebook page. She's *in*. After three or four months, though, her attendance gets sporadic and quickly peters out. I reach out to her via email, text, Twitter message, carrier pigeon, anything to find out what happened, but I get no response. Eva, for whatever reason, has decided she's not interested in Urban Village any more.

When we first launched worship, this kind of interaction would really bother me. I couldn't figure out why a person who had pledged their faithfulness and loyalty to the church would leave so quickly. We know how important it is to connect newcomers so that they build relationships with other people. That's huge in fostering stickiness in a church. But even when you attempt to do that, it's impossible to know how or why someone like Eva leaves. The unpredictability can be maddening, which is why I like the certainty of crossword puzzles now. And it's also why this text from Luke has become one of my favorites.

This passage is one of the lectionary texts for Thanksgiving Day, so I would imagine when pastors preach on it, they offer gratitude as a main theme. The text never had much of an impact on me before becoming a church planter. In the last few years, though, it's become my go-to Scripture story when people flake out. As Jesus enters a village, ten lepers approach him, begging to be healed. They must have shouted because they were far away from Jesus (lepers were required to keep a certain distance from others because of their uncleanness), but their desire was clear: "Jesus, Master, have mercy on us!"

Jesus starts them on the process toward healing, off they go to the priests, and, indeed, they are made clean. A miracle! If there had been a local coffee shop ("Holy Grounds," maybe?) in this village, one would hope that many of them would have sat down with Jesus to tell him how their lives had been changed. But only one did. And here's where the lesson in gratitude enters a preacher's sermon, because this one individual shows us the proper way to express thanks. It's a good lesson. It makes sense. But something different struck me when I read it after becoming a church planter.

People were fickle even with Jesus!

That's my takeaway anyway. In today's church world, which likes to measure many things, a 10 percent return rate on a particular ministry wouldn't be anything to brag about. I can imagine a supervisor sitting down with Jesus: "So, Jesus, you set everything up correctly. Well done on getting people in the door, listening to their felt needs, and addressing them. But what happened after that? Did you sign them up for small groups right away? I'm concerned about your stickiness factor."

Jesus' comments after the one leper came back probably bespeak the lesson in giving thanks and praise that he was trying to convey: "Were not ten made clean? But the other nine, where are they? Was none of them found to return and give praise to God except this foreigner?" (Luke 17:17). Part of me hopes, though, that a tiny part of Jesus was genuinely puzzled by the lack of return. The other nine. Where were they? I doubt Jesus lost a lot of sleep over this, but it's kind of comforting for me to imagine that he got frustrated at this "failure."

Like the vast majority of East Germans, Alexandra was raised in an atheistic family. It was only as a young adult that she began to show an interest in the Christian faith. After a couple of months attending our church, we all were delighted when Alexandra made a faith commitment and asked to be baptized.

Her special day came and the church was packed with visitors, including many of Alexandra's family members and friends, who were in a church for the first time in their lives. All was going according to plan as we progressed through the liturgy of the worship service until I actually turned to the baptismal font to baptize Alexandra . . . and there was no water in it! I had failed to check this before the service. I have done so every time since!

—Barry Sloan
Director of Evangelism for The United Methodist Church in Germany
Author, *When the Saints Go Marching: On the Trail of Columbanus*

When you think about it in twenty-first-century church terms, Jesus failed on all aspects of the stickiness factor. For example, he knew how to draw a crowd, but it seems like he also repelled people quite often, too. One of the most notable instances happened at the very beginning of his public ministry. Church planters are often taught to have big launches for their ministries, and Jesus appeared to do this. Luke 4:14 tells us that he returned to Galilee, began to teach, and was praised by everyone. A great beginning! But then he started quoting the prophets and talked about the poor and blind and oppressed. He quickly challenged the authorities and ticked off people he should have been courting. Instead of drawing people into his ministry, he drove them away! "They got up, drove him out of the town, and led him to the brow of the hill on which their town was built, so that they might hurl him off the cliff," says Luke 4:29. I've had more than a few Sundays when worship numbers were pretty low, but I don't think it ever reached the point when people threatened Preacher Cliff-Throwing.

I share this not to disparage the importance of metrics or gathering large crowds, but merely to point out that, if you think about it, Jesus had his share of what society (and the church) might call failures. What was important to him was not building a false community for the sake of boosting his denominational statistic reports, but being true to his nature and calling. It just so happens that his nature of being fully divine and fully human is different from yours or mine, but his authenticity outshines his failures. Authenticity is a buzzword in ministry these days, but you can't escape the fact that young adult after young adult tells me that they want their spiritual leaders to be *real,* true to who they are. Part of being truthful is being transparent about your failures.

Note that Jesus named the fact that only one returned and then uses this as a teaching moment. Transparent. Authentic. The text doesn't tell us exactly who he's talking to, but I don't think he was just talking to the Samaritan who returned. I believe he's talking to us, as well. He's open about all aspects of his ministry. We should be, too, so that others can see that unmet expectations do not end our ministry hopes.

The Parable of the Sower (Mark 4:1-9)

Flipping a pancake wouldn't appear to be the most difficult job in the world, but I apparently didn't have the right wrist action to pull it off. I needed to find a job the summer before my senior year of college (yes, the same summer I worked selling shoes to children at a department store), and an opportunity I thought would be perfect fell through. I panicked a bit and took the first job that came along: working under the golden arches of McDonald's on Merle Hay Road in Urbandale, Iowa. Not as any kind of corporate intern, but flipping burgers while listening to my sixteen-year-old supervisor bark orders at me. Working behind a grill never came naturally to me, and that included one morning when I was making pancakes. I did my best to keep up with the orders, but in the process of flipping one of the pancakes, it came out a little misshapen. Instead of a golden round circle, it looked a little like a kidney bean that had been stepped on. My supervisor just happened to be walking by and stopped to look at the sad, broken pancake.

"What happened here?" he asked.

"I broke it," I said, stating the obvious.

"Let me ask you something," he replied (I knew a brief lecture was coming my way). "If you were a customer, would you want to eat that pancake?"

I was tempted to say, when I eat a McDonald's pancake, I really couldn't care less about the shape, as long as it tastes OK and is hidden by a sausage patty. Instead, I dutifully answered no, and that pancake made its way into the garbage. I knew I wouldn't be long for that job.

I mention my lack of success as a McDonald's employee as a way to introduce the parable Jesus told in Mark 4. A large crowd had gathered around Jesus at the edge of the sea as he taught from a boat. He shared a story about a sower who sowed seed, which landed in a variety of places: a path, rocky ground, among thorns, and, finally good soil. Jesus explained the parable by drawing parallels between the varieties of ground and our lives and hearts—how we receive the word that is sown.

It wasn't until I was a church planter, though, that another meaning became clear to me. This sower was a lousy farmer! Wouldn't it make more sense for him to carefully look for the good soil first? Why waste your time in sowing seed on a path or among thorns? If the sower had sower colleagues, I'm sure they must have snickered at him.

But I admire this sower's chutzpah, and maybe he wasn't as bad a farmer as I first thought. We can't fully intuit his planting intentions, but it seems to me that he could have played it safe and only made sure that he planted in good soil. He had to know that sowing on a path or on rocky ground didn't make much sense, didn't he? He took a chance, though, and "wasted" a few seeds, just in case. There's something to be said for sowing seed in places where others say it won't work (and for taking that to heart as we think about places in our communities where we think people won't receive the gospel).

Again, I imagine he came home from a day of sowing, and maybe his wife asked how his day went.

"Oh, not very well," he might have replied. "I kept throwing the seed on concrete. I'm not sure that's going to work."

His supportive wife may have encouraged him while she also wondered, what is wrong with this guy? The sower probably went to bed that night and thought, "Maybe I'm not cut out for this job."

But here's the key to the passage for me as it relates to failure: *The sower kept sowing.* Three times, he tried his hand at this, and three times he came home, having failed at his task.

But he keeps sowing. The fourth time he tried? Jackpot. I realize this may not be the central point of the text (and I'm taking some liberties in assuming that he did this over several days rather than in one day), but it's enormously helpful when thinking about failing. Here's a farmer whose expertise had to be questioned by others, but no one can doubt the one thing that eventually brought about a harvest: his faithfulness.

A religious leader's faith can move from solid to fragile when taking risks and attempting to start new ministries. When those efforts bring little to no fruit, it's tempting to doubt yourself and also to doubt God's ability to do new things in your context. The sower did an interesting thing here, though. Not only did he continue to sow, but he also changed some things.

He started on the path. Maybe no one had tried sowing here before, he thought. Maybe some of the seeds could get into the cracks. Something within him moved him to give it a shot. He did, it didn't work, and then he went to the thorny ground. Maybe something would be able to grow in this environment? he asked himself. He tried it, it didn't work, and he moved on one more time. The point here is that, yes, he continued to sow, but he also learned as he went. He didn't let an initial failure stop him from sowing, and it also didn't stop him from sowing in a place that others said wouldn't work. Just because others said it was dumb to sow there didn't mean that he couldn't at least try.

We can learn a few things from this sower. First, have faith in yourself that you have been led by God to sow the word in places that others have either tried or have said, don't bother. Try it. Throw a few seeds. See what happens. It may not work, but just because it fails doesn't mean you hang up your seed bag (or whatever it is that sowers put seeds in). Another lesson is to learn from the failure. If sowing the seed in a new place doesn't seem to be bearing any fruit, try a different place, even yet another place that others say won't work. Remember, the sower tried three different areas to see where his seeds would take root. The seeds won't take root along a path? Duly noted. Among thorns? Got it. In the heat? Good to know. No one said you should risk and fail only once. Whether you're breaking pancakes or wasting seeds, sometimes you have to fail repeatedly in order to improve your flipping skills or discover the context that best fits your ministry.

Peter Drowns (Matthew 14:22-33)

Several years ago, the TV personality David Letterman was honored at Ball State University, his alma mater in Muncie, Indiana. The school decided to name its new telecommunications building after him, and Letterman returned to Muncie, making several self-deprecating remarks along the way. His ironic sense of humor had made its way to Ball State before. A plaque was already on a wall of the school's Department of Telecommunications that was dedicated to Letterman. Most plaques pay tribute to an individual's great accomplishments or a sizable financial donation, but this plaque was different. It was from Letterman and was dedicated "to all 'C' students before and after me!"

It's rare for a public statue or plaque to name anything other than rousing success. I think of my times spent traveling in Europe and visiting numerous churches and cathedrals, many of which house statues of our ancestors of the faith. They're often larger than life, crafted with expert care and cold, smooth materials, and placed above us, so that we can look up and be inspired. While these monuments of creativity can be moving, they don't always tell the whole story.

We may have become used to the fact that the gospels (especially Mark) didn't portray the disciples in the best light. That the gospel writers chose to reveal these marks of imperfection speak to the authenticity of these stories. The gospel writers had little love for hagiographies. Yet we still need to be reminded, I think, that these early followers of Jesus failed in numerous ways. This story from Matthew 14 is a good example.

This is Peter's first big moment in Matthew. He's mentioned individually three times before this passage: When Jesus invited Peter to follow him in chapter 4, when Jesus entered Peter's house and healed his mother-in-law in chapter 8, and when he is mentioned as one of the twelve apostles in chapter 10. We don't get a sense of Peter's real importance—when Jesus declared Peter will be the one upon whom the church will be built—until Matthew 16, the story when Jesus walked on the water, which came immediately after the story when Jesus fed the five thousand.

After this memorable feast, the disciples got into a boat, while Jesus went up to a mountain to pray. A strong wind comes up, which took the boat (sans Jesus) out into the sea. Early the next morning, Jesus walked on the water out to them. Many of the disciples reported a ghost sighting until Jesus assured them that he was no ghost. Here's where Peter entered the scene. How did Peter do when the spotlight shone on him? Not bad at first. With more than a little *chutzpah*, Peter said, "Lord, if it is you, command me to come to you on the water." The text doesn't specify Jesus' reaction, but I'd like to believe he admired Peter's courage. Jesus invited him out onto the water: "Come."

The text also doesn't tell us if Peter looked to his left and then to his right and then pointed to himself and mouthed, "Me?" to Jesus, but he again gets points because he took a risk by getting out of the boat and making his way toward Jesus. That fickle (providential?) wind whipped up again, however, and provided a challenge to Peter, who became frightened, began to sink, and cried out, "Lord, save me!"

It's impossible to know the tone of Jesus' chastisement of Peter. The text tells us that Jesus wondered why Peter had such little faith. Maybe he said it not as a scold, but with a *you're-better-than-this* tone. I believe so, as Jesus placed a lot of trust in him not long after this incident (Matthew 16:18-19a: "And I tell you, you are Peter, and on this rock, I will build my church, and the gates of Hades will not prevail against it. I will give you the keys of the kingdom of heaven").

But before we jump ahead, let's also give Peter some credit for knowing to whom he should cry out when he had a (literally) sinking feeling. Peter didn't yell back to his buddies. He didn't try to swim on his own. He "failed" this test of faith, and rather than being stubborn about it, he admitted it was Jesus who would save him.

Because Urban Village is a multi-site church, I'm blessed to work with an amazing team of colleagues. I can't imagine doing ministry any other way. I'm also blessed to have what I consider my own little support team (including my wife, my counselor, my spiritual director, and my ministry coach), so I know I always have many people to turn to when the waves get particularly rough. I'm a little chagrined, though, when I think about how often I call out to them *first*. Not that there's anything particularly wrong with this because they never fail to provide a listening ear, an encouraging word, and wise counsel. But I sometimes wonder if maybe Jesus is in the corner, clearing his throat and saying, "You know, you could come to *me* first. I might have a few things to offer, too."

I'm sure the other disciples would have pitched in to help Peter, and they probably swung the boat around so a couple of them could haul him in. Yes, Peter may have started to drown, but at least he knew a thing or two about who to call first when he needed to be saved.

I always find it a little heart-warming to read about the disciples' failures. This particular story isn't necessarily just about one man's failure, though. It's a lesson in what initial step to take when you *are* drowning.

There are numerous statues of Peter throughout the world, but I wonder if an artist has ever tried to sculpt him flailing in water? Rather than placed high above us, a monument would be best located at ground level as a reminder that this man didn't always get it right. Maybe someday, someone will create a waterproof sculpture that combines water and a humble Peter as a life-saving lesson.

Martha Does It Wrong (Luke 10:38-42)

My kindergarten classmate Mary Murphy looked closely at my handiwork. We were doing a craft of sorts (I think it was an Easter basket . . . or maybe a May Day basket . . . it was some kind of basket) in our class. We were only supposed to make a cut halfway up a certain line and, for some reason, I cut much farther along the line, thereby *ruining* my basket. "Ooh," said Mary. "You're doing it wrong." I was never very good at art projects, and I was angry with Mary for pointing this out and also angry with myself for just not being able to follow directions.

My reaction to getting it wrong was probably a harbinger of my writing this book about failure. I've always hated to get it wrong. I don't know if it's because I'm a first-born child or if it says something about my Enneagram type. Who knows? But when I realize I have not followed the directions correctly (and especially when this fact is pointed out to me), the blood still rushes to my face. Imagine, then, what it must feel like when *Jesus* says you did it wrong.

Well, he didn't say it exactly that way, but still, here's an example from the gospel of Luke: "Martha, Martha, you are worried and distracted by many things; there is need of only one thing. Mary has chosen the better part, which will not be taken away from her" (Luke 10:41-42).

Oh, the sermons and reflections that have been shared about this story! There are so many ways Martha could have responded. Maybe she was humble and said, "Yes, Lord, you're right. I should learn from my sister." Maybe. But I kinda doubt it. I see Martha as somebody who also hates to get it wrong, don't you? Maybe she also resents Mary a little bit, as if this kind of comparison has happened before. "Oh, Martha," her mother might have said, "why aren't you more like your sister?"

I can see Martha trying to keep a stiff upper lip and later going to her room to either cry in frustration or punch a few pillows or just stew silently. I can relate. When I sit and stew, when I feel like Jesus has done me wrong, or if I feel like Jesus has said, "You've done it wrong," it's really hard to reflect on the fact that Jesus is trying to *help*.

There are a couple of things to notice here. Jesus pointed out something to Martha that's pretty obvious: You're distracted by many things. He then told her there's only one thing you need to pay attention to. Me.

This story of Mary and Martha only appears in Luke. Not long after this story in chapter 12, Luke included Jesus' teaching about worrying and anxiety, which is also found in the Sermon on the Mount in Matthew. After he reflected on the ravens of the air and lilies of the field, Jesus came to a similar conclusion in both teachings. Matthew's version goes like this:

Therefore do not worry, saying "What will we eat?" or "What will we drink?" or "What will we wear?" For it is the Gentiles who strive for all these things; and indeed your heavenly Father knows that you need all these things. But strive first for the kingdom of God and his righteousness, and all these things will be given to you as well.

Matthew 6:31-33

Luke's version is almost identical.

We don't know exactly what Jesus said to Mary as she sat at his feet, but maybe it was a preview of this teaching. And lo and behold, Martha needed to hear it, too.

A great scene in the movie *City Slickers* illustrates this well. *City Slickers* is a movie about three city-dwellers who try to get away from it all on a week-long trip to a working ranch in the West. Billy Crystal's character (Mitch) is going through a midlife crisis of sorts and trying to find meaning in his life. While riding on a horse one day, he receives a simple bit of wisdom from Curly, one of the veteran ranchers and guides for the "campers."

"You know what the secret of life is?" Curly asks Mitch as Curly holds up one finger.

Mitch jokingly answers, "Your finger?"

"One thing. Just one thing. You stick to that and everything else don't mean s***."

"That's great, but . . . what's the one thing?" asks Mitch.

"That's what you gotta figure out," Curly responds.

We don't exactly know what Martha's one thing was, but I think Jesus sensed that she could choose a better option. It may have been hard for Martha to hear this because the one thing she chose (having a reputation as a great host?) seemed to have ended in failure. But notice that Jesus didn't say that Mary *is* better. Only that Mary had *chosen* better. There's a big difference. Failure has that sneaky way of telling you just the opposite: that your actions equate with your worth.

Jesus tried to use Martha's "failure" as an opportunity to teach her to rethink her choices and priorities. Jesus clearly loved Martha. (I love how he uses her name twice in verse 41. I believe it was said with fondness and not disapproval or annoyance.) He simply wanted her to think less of saving face and more of saving her soul.

What's your one thing? It's important to remember that your one thing isn't ultimately the worship attendance of the congregation you serve or the admiration of your peers. Similar to Peter knowing that it was Jesus that he should call out to first, and Mary knowing that it was Jesus that she should spend most of her time with, this story reminds us of what (or, rather, Who) our one thing should be.

Zechariah Asked the Wrong Question (Luke 1:5-25)

I don't know if PBS had a feeling that its popular English drama *Downton Abbey* would be a success, but once it was, I'm sure executives were trying to figure out, "How can we capitalize on this? How can we convert Downton Abbey fans into fans of the whole Masterpiece series?" Whatever they did worked on my wife and me. We went from watching public television only when our young son watched the PBS show *Arthur* to getting hooked on *Downtown Abbey* to faithfully dedicating our Sunday evenings to anything Masterpiece put out. Part of the Masterpiece family is "Masterpiece Mysteries." I had never been a particular fan of mystery novels or TV shows, but it's become kind of fun to watch and try to figure out who the culprit is. I'm still a novice at this virtual detective work, so I'm more often wrong than right, but I always try to pay particular attention to characters one would normally overlook.

When I was reflecting on "failure" stories in the gospels, the story of Elizabeth struck me as a possibility. Surely she must have been seen as a failure in her circles because of her inability to conceive. In Luke 1:25, she said as much after she finally did get pregnant: "This is what the Lord has done for me when he looked favorably on me and took away the disgrace I have endured among my people." In this story, however, I had always overlooked one of the other characters: Zechariah. When it finally dawned on me that he may also have "failed," I wondered (like trying to figure out who the culprit is in a mystery) how I had missed it.

Zechariah surely must have had a stellar reputation in his community. He was a priest who belonged to the order of Abijah and was married to a woman who also came from a priestly family. The couple was righteous and blameless, following all the commandments and regulations they were supposed to follow. Here's one of those big "buts" of the Bible, however. After Luke 1:5-6 summarizes how failure-proof they seemingly should have been, verse 7 intones: "But they had no children." In the *New Interpreter's Bible*, R. Alan Culpepper summarizes their situation starkly: "Barrenness was regarded as a tragedy, a disgrace, and even a sign of God's punishment."[5]

No doubt this inability to conceive plunged them both into darkness, and they did what most faithful people do: prayed like crazy. Zechariah followed his priestly duties, entered the sanctuary of the Lord, and offered incense. Little did he know that his and Elizabeth's lives are about to be transformed. An angel appeared to foretell joy and gladness. They will have a son!

I have to believe that up until this point, Zechariah had been constantly questioning himself. What did I do to deserve this?

How have I failed? The euphoria of this vision, however, must have erased all those questions. He went from despair to elation as he heard this amazing news. There was just one thing, though, and he couldn't help himself. He (like many of us would have done) asked a question. A modern rendering of the story may go something like this:

"Uh, Lord? I'm unbelievably thankful for this visit and this news. You, more than anyone, know just how painful these years of childlessness have been. Just one question. I don't mean to seem ungrateful or anything, but, well, you know, I just don't see . . . *how*. Elizabeth and I are old, and this whole thing will probably seem unbelievable to many . . ."

The angel (now identified as Gabriel) probably had a look of disbelief. What is up with this guy? He received this amazing gift. Why couldn't he just accept it? Gabriel decided that probably the best thing Zechariah needed was a time-out of sorts. To be silent. To listen. Maybe even to receive a grander vision of who God is. It's impossible for us to know Zechariah's concept of God. Clearly he was faithful, even righteous. But, as Rev. John Buchanan writes, maybe Gabriel saw Zechariah's question as a lack of imagination, rather than doubt: "Barbara Brown Taylor suggests that Zechariah's sin was not so much doubt and disbelief as 'a failure of imagination . . . a habit of hopelessness.'"[6] Zechariah is the one who is truly barren because he cannot imagine a different future, cannot entertain something new and hopeful." Maybe silence was just the right prescription for him so that he could later receive a grander, more unpredictable notion of who God is and what God can do.

But poor Zechariah! He already may have been feeling like a failure, because he and Elizabeth couldn't conceive, and now he can't even respond to miraculous news correctly. Silence, however, was probably the best thing for him.

I played baseball in high school and was a decent pitcher. One of my shortcomings, however, was control. I always liked to throw the ball as fast and as hard as I possibly could, which meant that I ~~occasionally~~ often threw more balls than strikes. There was one game when I walked quite a few batters, but not many of them scored, so the game was close. Near the end of the game, though, I was gassed, and the coach came to take me out. No pitcher likes to get taken out of the game, and so I sulked as I walked off the mound and into the dugout. I don't remember exactly what happened next, but the pitcher the coach wanted to bring in wasn't ready, and so the coach looked at me in the dugout and said, "Do you want to give it another try?"

If you're not familiar with baseball, this is a pretty rare thing—for a pitcher to get taken out only to get a chance to go back in. I was a competitor and was discouraged that I hadn't pitched better so, of course, I said, "Yes, coach!" I made my way back in and onto the mound and faced the next batter, determined to lead our team to victory.

Wouldn't it be a great story if I struck that batter out and our team ended up getting the win? Instead, literally on my first pitch, I threw it way outside, the ball skipped past the catcher and the leading run scored from third. The coach realized he had made a mistake in sending me back out there and promptly took me out again. This time, for good.

What does this story have to do with Zechariah? Sometimes when we fail (or perceive that we fail), it's tempting to want to keep trying harder. We tense our muscles up or squeeze our eyes so that our brains go into overdrive to make up for what we did wrong. But what we really need is time away. To reflect. To pray. To listen. To change *silent* from an adjective into a verb, as in, "I'm going to silent today." To do nothing and let God have a say and act accordingly.

John Francis is an environmentalist with a particular expertise in the impact oil spills can have on the environment. What he's really known for, though, is his seventeen-year self-imposed vow to neither talk nor drive or ride in motorized vehicles as a way to bring attention to the plight of the planet. After the seventeen years, he realized that the time had come when he would have a bigger impact by talking about his experiences and what he learned. (He jokes that his mother shouted, "Hallelujah, Johnny's talking!" when he broke his silence.) He's understandably received attention for his vow of silence (how can someone go *seventeen* years without talking?), but in watching a TED talk of his, I was struck by his observations on how this time of silence made him a better listener. In his autobiography *Planetwalker,* Francis notes, "Most of my adult life I have not been listening fully. I only listened long enough to determine whether the speaker's ideas matched my own. If they didn't, I would stop listening, and my mind would race ahead to compose an argument against what I believed the speaker's idea or position to be."[7]

In order for him to really understand something that he thought he knew a lot about—the environment—he had to stop jumping to conclusions and responding as if he had all the answers. He had to simply listen to what others were saying. His silence opened and broadened his perspective. In his TED talk, Francis describes what happened that first day he decided not to talk:

> So on this first day I actually listened. And it was very sad for me, because I realized that for those many years I had not been learning. I was 27. I thought I knew everything. I didn't. And so I decided I'd better do this for another day, and another day, and another day until finally, I promised myself for a year I would keep quiet because I started learning more and more and I needed to learn more.

So for a year I said I would keep quiet, and then on my birthday I would reassess what I had learned and maybe I would talk again. Well, that lasted 17 years.[8]

Zechariah never did anything wrong, and he wasn't being punished, per se. He simply needed a greater understanding of what God could do, and the only way that was going to happen was for him to close his mouth and open his heart and ears. Maybe because of the silence, Zechariah did some deep reflection and emptied himself. This allowed the Holy Spirit to fill him so that he could later utter the powerful prophecy in Luke 1:67-79, which ends with these words: "By the tender mercy of our God, the dawn from on high will break upon us, to give light to those who sit in darkness and in the shadow of death, to guide our feet into the way of peace" (Luke 1:78-79).

As I think back to my kindergarten self, I realize that I probably had an issue with listening closely to directions, which may be why, when it came to paper-basket creation, I "did it wrong." But sometimes doing it wrong can lead to deep moments of silence and reflection, and out of that comes new insights and creations.

Disciples Fell Asleep on the Job (Mark 14:32-42)

One of my favorite follows on Twitter is @JustHadOneJob. I'm not sure who actually creates these, but somebody takes the time to find on-the-job failures and then puts pictures of these failures online. The emphasis, of course, is on failures that seemingly could have been avoided: You had one job to do, and you messed it up! An example is a photo of half a cabbage wrapped in cellophane at a grocery store. The sticker that shows the price and the name of the product, however, says: "Watermelon, $2.49." You can imagine the admonishment: "You had one job: Put stickers that say 'Cabbage' on the products that are, you know, actual cabbages."

We've all been there. We have a simple task that we're supposed to complete, and yet, somehow, some way, it gets messed up. Which brings us to the gospel of Mark and the disciples.

As I noted in the section on Peter, one of the things that gives the gospels some historical authenticity is the fact that they are no hagiographies of the first followers of Jesus. The gospels give us unvarnished looks at these twelve men, and Mark handed out the barbs especially freely.

One example comes from Mark 8:14-21. Jesus and the disciples had just gotten into a boat after a wearying exchange with some Pharisees, but someone missed the assignment to pack lunch:

> When Christian asked me about failures, one quickly came to mind. When we first started Community we had a midweek service . . . Remember those? We try not to remember them either. We were holding ours one time each month on a Wednesday evening. We wanted to add another one in order to give people another opportunity for extended worship and teaching, but we were afraid that putting the second one on another Wednesday night would crush all our small groups that met on Wednesdays. So we came up with the idea to hold one on the first Wednesday and another on the third Thursday. Or was it the first Thursday and third Wednesday? You get the picture. That was not a brilliant idea; more like a colossal failure. It resulted in complete confusion, and no one could ever remember when to show up for the midweek service.
>
> —Jon Ferguson
> Co-Founder of Community Christian Church
> Author, *Starting Over: Your Life Beyond Regrets*

"Now the disciples had forgotten to bring any bread; and they had only one loaf with them in the boat." Jesus, as he often does, used this as a teaching moment and compared the bread to the yeast of the Pharisees. The disciples, bless their hearts, think that Jesus is still talking about the lunch bread.

So here we have a Jesus who was exasperated by the Pharisees and had just been given a reminder that these guys he chose are still novices at this whole faith thing, and he's not thrilled. Why, he wants to know, are you still talking about this freaking bread? Let's pick it up in the middle of verse 17: "Do you still not perceive or understand? Are your hearts hardened? Do you have eyes, and fail to see? Do you have ears, and fail to hear?"

To be fair, sometimes the disciples *did* get it. Not long after this exchange, Peter answered correctly ("You are the Messiah") after Jesus quizzed them about his identity. But they have more than their share of screw-ups, including one right before Jesus is arrested.

Jesus took Peter, James, and John with him to Gethsemane, a place to pray, but also a place of stress and pressure (the word Gethsemane, interestingly, means "oil press"). Jesus gave the three disciples one job to do. Well, two actually: One, remain here. Two, keep awake. That's it. Jesus was experiencing distress and agitation, and he wanted his friends to support him while he went and heart-wrenchingly shared his deep desires with God. After doing so, he returned, and Mark 14:37 described the situation simply: "He came and found them sleeping." Maybe Jesus muttered under his breath, "You had one job." The fact that they fell asleep two more times adds a little macabre humor to the text.

I'm very grateful for the inclusion of stories like this one in the gospels, because it displays the disciples' humanity and draws me closer to these fellow followers of Jesus. What may have exacerbated their sense of failure was Jesus' arrest right after this scene.

Not only didn't they do what Jesus asked but now, they must have assumed, they wouldn't have a chance to restore the relationship. The perceived finality of this failure must have weighed on them.

I think many of us have had an experience of having a supervisor (or maybe it was a teacher or even a parent) who had little patience for mistakes. One screw-up and you'd get yelled at or even fired. That, of course, only intensifies the anxiety in that particular situation. I had an experience similar to this.

Remember the summer job where I packed explosives? As I mentioned, it wasn't the most intellectually stimulating work I'd ever had. I always showed up on time and never left early, but I certainly didn't have a peppy attitude that screamed, "I would pack explosives without getting paid because this job is just that awesome!" I'm sure I shuffled my feet at times, and I wasn't above taking quick naps on breaks (although I never slept through a shift). Anyway, that lack of get-up-and-go apparently didn't go over well with the owner of the small company. I finished work for the summer in mid-August, and I went back one last time to pick up my paycheck. The owner invited me into his office, and I assumed we would have a "Thank you for working for us" kind of conversation. Instead, he said, "Chris, I'm glad you were able to make some money for college this summer, but I need to tell you something. If you had been a permanent worker, I probably would have fired you."

I was stunned. He went on to bemoan my aforementioned lack of zeal for the job and then rattled off examples of my supposed bad attitude. I couldn't believe it. Even though this wasn't technically a firing, it sure felt like it. I bewilderedly walked out of his office, feeling like a failure. As I thought about this conversation a few days later, I think the thing that upset me the most was that I had no idea he wasn't happy with my job performance and now I didn't have a chance to prove that I *was* a hard worker. He would forever think of me as a slacker, a failure at packing explosives. Of course, I wasn't planning on doing this for a career—it was a summer job, after all—but it still ate at me. The fact that I'm writing about this almost thirty years later is probably evidence that it still eats at me!

Among the many things I'm sure the disciples regretted after Jesus was arrested, this scene in Gethsemane had to have come up in their minds. Not only had they failed Jesus, but they had run out of chances to follow him, pray with him, eat with him. They couldn't prove that, yes, *they could stay awake.*

Thankfully, they discovered that more chances were coming their way. One of my favorite post-resurrection stories is told in John 21. We, of course, know the John 20 resurrection story when Jesus appears before Mary, as well as Jesus' poignant questions and commands to Peter in John 21:15-19 ("Do you love me? Feed my lambs"), are worthy of deep contemplation. But in John's telling of Jesus' resurrection appearances, I'm partial to John 21:7.

We learn from John 20 that Peter discovered that the body of Jesus was missing, and we know that the resurrected Jesus appeared before the disciples (which includes the Thomas' famous demands to see and feel the proof that it is indeed Jesus standing in front of them). John 20, however, doesn't tell us how Peter specifically *felt* about seeing the resurrected Jesus. This is where John 21 comes in.

At the beginning of this chapter, we see that Peter went back to what he knows: fishing. What's his mindset? Was he thrilled that he saw Jesus? Did he quite believe it? Did he wait in the background because of the shame of his failure to stay awake and his denial that he even knew Jesus? Talk about compounding failures! What we know is this: He returned to the familiar. He went out on the water with close companions. He sat there all night long and kept throwing out the nets and bringing them back in with nothing to show for it. I can imagine with each empty net, Peter muttered, "Figures." Then one of the disciples caught a glimpse of a bystander on the shore who shared a little fishing advice: "Try the other side of the boat!" the bystander yelled. The bonanza of fish they caught opened their eyes, and they soon realized that the bystander is Jesus.

There is no doubting Peter's reaction this time: "When Simon Peter heard it was the Lord, he wrapped his coat around himself (for he was naked) and jumped into the water. The other disciples followed in the boat" (John 21:7b-8a, CEB). Another chance. And Peter literally leapt at this new opportunity.

My dad recently retired from his second career as a United Methodist pastor, but before he went into the ministry in the early 1990s, he worked as an educator for many years. Early in his career, he taught physical education and coached cross-country, wrestling, and track in the small Iowa town where we lived. He told me a story the other day about Tim, one of the wrestlers on his team, who recently reached out to thank him for the impact my dad on his life. This particular wrestler didn't have a very impressive resume. His physique was less than stellar, and he also "wrestled up" a weight class most of the season, meaning he was competing against other wrestlers who weighed more than he did. He lost nearly all of his matches. My dad kept wondering if it made sense for them to keep sending Tim out there, but the young man was determined to keep at it. Every match was a new opportunity, and he got his one victory near the end of the season after he had lost time after time.

Tim is now a teacher and as part of a staff development exercise, he and his colleagues were asked to write a letter to a role model to thank them. Tim wrote my dad to thank him for not giving up on him through all the losses. He remembered the tough workouts and said he learned a lot about discipline and hard work, and how it had now helped him as a teacher and mentor.

Can you imagine? Losing all of those matches and yet eagerly anticipating the next one, believing, "This is the one." I share this not as a run-of-the-mill story about perseverance but to highlight some people's willingness to take chances after failure. That can be one of the toughest things to do. Failure can kill the desire to risk again, because we don't want to go through the pain of screwing up or letting someone down. But the will to say yes to new opportunities in the face of failing again cannot be overlooked. James 1:25 sums up my belief in the necessity of perseverance: "But those who look into the perfect law, the law of liberty, and persevere, being not hearers who forget but doers who act—they will be blessed in their doing."

Grace comes as second, third, and fourth chances. Jesus gave Peter new opportunities, too. After consistently asking about the steadfastness of Peter's love, he gives him three more chances to serve and be faithful. "Feed my lambs," Jesus said, in John 21:15. Later, Jesus adds, "Tend my sheep" and "Feed my sheep" to the new opportunities that Peter has before him.

After telling me the story about Tim, my dad made the observation that he never heard from the wrestlers who were successful. It was the one who failed who perhaps appreciated the lessons that failure and new opportunities offered to him. May we have the same exuberant perseverance that Peter and this wrestler showed in our own ministries.

4

HOW TO SUCCEED
WHILE FAILING

Though "cowpox" seems like a great name for a punk band, it doesn't sound like something you'd want to spend a lot of time around. This disease, however, was influential in the discovery of what is considered the first vaccination.

Edward Jenner was a scientist and surgeon in Great Britain in the late eighteenth and early nineteenth century. At the time, cowpox was a relatively harmless disease that individuals contracted when coming in contact with, naturally, cows. The story goes that a local milkmaid told Jenner something remarkably coincidental: People who contracted cowpox never contracted smallpox, a much more serious—and deadly—disease. Jenner must have filed this away in his mind, because later he treated Sarah Nelmes, another dairymaid who had contracted cowpox.

Jenner saw this as an opportunity to test the theory that cowpox carriers were immune to smallpox viruses. Though we would be appalled at Jenner's testing methods today, he took James Phipps, the eight-year old son of his gardener, made some scratches on the boy's arm, and rubbed material from one of the pocks on Nelmes' hand into the boy's scratches. The boy did contract cowpox, but recovered a week later.

Jenner then took the next step of practicing variolation, a technique not uncommon among doctors of the day, in which they introduced the smallpox virus to a body as a way to combat it. Variolation was an inexact science at the time, however, and caused some deaths. As a way to test his own theory, Jenner variolated young James to see if the introduction of the cowpox virus antibodies would combat the smallpox virus. His experiment worked. Jenner followed up with other experiments and then published his findings in that classic summer-beach read, "An Inquiry into the Causes and Effects of the Variolae Vaccinae; a Disease Discovered in some of the Western Counties of England, Particularly Gloucestershire, and Known by the Name of The Cow Pox." All kidding aside, Jenner is known today as the inventor of the vaccination.

I've only recently started getting a flu shot every year, and I suppose one reason I resisted is because the whole process seemed incongruous to me. *You're injecting the virus into my body?* I know the science of it (and by "know," I mean I have a first-grade-level understanding): The inoculation introduces a weakened virus into my body, which produces antibodies to protect me from a stronger flu virus. But it still seems a little odd.

The vaccination metaphor is the best one I can come up with to introduce a concept that may seem even more odd, especially to an American audience: Integrating small failures (like the cowpox virus) into our ministries can help stave off more critical failures (like the smallpox virus) in your church's future. In fact, what may result is renewed and unexpected church health in areas you weren't expecting. Here's an example from my church.

One of our favorite Urban Village stories about the unexpected benefits of failure occurred in the summer of 2010, three months after we had launched worship at our first site. One of our core values is to be inclusive, which means creating truly welcoming spaces for all, including LGBTQ individuals. One of the best ways we know how to do that is not to simply wait for folks to walk into our various worship and small-group spaces so we can welcome them but to also go out into the streets and practice gospel hospitality wherever we are. Walking in Chicago's Pride Parade is a good example of this.

Every year on the last Sunday of June, an estimated one million people line the streets in Chicago's Uptown, Lakeview, and Lincoln Park neighborhoods to cheer for the parade's numerous LGBTQ-affirming groups and floats. We're proud to walk with numerous faith groups in the parade, and we always try to be particularly bold (another of our core values) when we do so by handing out small flyers that proclaim God loves all and, truth be told, also give some information about our church.

I'll never forget the first year we walked. We handed out hundreds of flyers along the parade route, and I thought for sure this would be a great way to publicize Urban Village. I couldn't wait for the next Sunday to arrive, because I just knew many people would see our flyers and flock to our church. I wondered: Should we print more bulletins to be ready? Recruit extra greeters? The day arrived and we flung open the doors to . . . about the same number of people that had already been coming. The same thing happened the Sunday after that one and the Sunday after that one. There was no bump in attendance and, on the bulletin slips that we encourage visitors to fill out, no one said they came because of the parade. I kind of considered that initial Pride Parade evangelism effort a waste of time and money. Thankfully, my mind has drastically changed.

We've now walked in the parade for six straight years, and I'm sure we've handed out at least 10,000 flyers. In all that time, we've maybe had ten people attend an Urban Village event or worship because of a flyer. And that may be generous. If you look at the rate of return (one-tenth of one percent), it would be a failure by any standard of measurement.

So why do we keep integrating this kind of failure into our evangelism plan every year? We discovered an unexpected benefit, and you can see it in the pictures of UVCers who walk every year. We had about a dozen people walk that first year, and now more than one hundred do. Participation has increased not just because we've grown, but because word has spread about the personal impact the parade has on those who walk. You can see it in their faces and hear it in their stories. Here's one from Eric:

> I moved to Chicago three years ago. I came to this city as a twenty-eight-year-old Christian and a three-year-old out gay man. I had found friction in my recent experiences out of the closet as I tried to marry the two sides of myself: a gay man and a Christian man. Marching in this parade made me uncomfortable. It put a spotlight on this tear inside myself. It pushed my boundaries and encouraged me, once again, to come out of the closet; this time, it was the Christian closet. Passing out flyers about Urban Village to bystanders was odd. Each time I did so, I was letting people know that I was a Christian. There is something remarkable about coming out of such closets. Taking this leap of faith, no matter how large or how small clarifies the relationship you have with witnesses of your

"coming out" experience. With these tiny interactions on the Halsted Street side of "Boystown," my UVC flyers were accepted with warmth and invitation. "Yes, you are gay. Yes, you are a Christian. Yes, I accept your flyer. Yes, you are welcome here."

I compare the impact it has on the walkers to the reaction of the seventy who were sent out by Jesus. In Luke 10:1-12, Jesus appoints "seventy others" to go ahead of him to every town and place and bring peace, cure the sick, and proclaim that the kingdom of God is near. They do so, and verse 17 records their excitement: "The seventy returned with joy, saying, 'Lord, in your name even the demons submit to us!'" The text doesn't tell us if the seventy initially went out with excitement and joy. Maybe some of them were pumped up, but I have to believe that some of them went a little grudgingly, not because they didn't believe in what Jesus came to do, but because this may have been taking them way out of their comfort zone. After actually participating, however, their hearts and minds were changed.

We've walked in the parade enough so I can now count on two things. One, hardly anyone will come to an Urban Village worship because of our flyers. Two, a whole lot of people who walk with Urban Village will come up to me, their faces flush with excitement, and say, "That was awesome!" This is particularly true of people who consider themselves introverted or shy. It's understandable that they would be apprehensive (*I'm* still apprehensive every year) because it's such a public exercise, but the excitement of the day, the cheering of the crowds, and, I believe, the Holy Spirit's submission of the demons of homophobia and exclusion has made them all evangelists. The parade is now pretty much a failure of a direct-marketing effort but has become an unparalleled evangelism training event for our members. If you're willing to wear bright colors and walk down the street handing out flyers about inclusion and literally yell to thousands of people, "God loves you!" all of a sudden, inviting your neighbor or co-worker to church doesn't seem so daunting. The gospel has gotten ahold of them, and they're eager to find new and creative ways to share this good news of reconciliation, restoration, and resurrection.

This is just one example of how we've integrated "failure" into our church in order to bring about unexpected blessings and immunize ourselves to larger and more critical failures, which include complacency and an overemphasis on taking care of and nurturing ourselves while we subconsciously ignore our neighbors.

It stings when we fail at trying new things in our churches, but that unpleasant feeling means that we are moving out of our comfort zones. It means we are willing to go to great lengths to share the timeless and life-changing message of Jesus' radical love, and, I believe, it means we're on the road to healthier ministries. A church that moves out of its comfort zone, more often than not, is a church that is attuned to the needs and desires of its neighborhood. It's understandable to be afraid of failure. However, if that fear paralyzes us and we don't risk anything, we may save ourselves the sting of failure, but I fear that we set ourselves up for the *real* pain of a church or ministry that has to close.

This was confirmed for me in a recent *Freakanomics* podcast. *Freakanomics: A Rogue Economist Explores The Hidden Side of Everything* was a hugely successful book in 2005, and it has spun off a cottage industry for the book's two authors, Steven Levitt and Stephen Dubner, including a podcast that is often the number-one download on the Apple iTunes store. The podcast's objective is the same as the book's: to explore the hidden side of everything. A recent episode was titled "How to Become Great at Just About Anything," and it included an interview with Dubner and Anders

> I will always remember a first meeting with a finance committee in my early years of ministry. I was young, nervous, and in over my head in so many ways. I wanted to prove that I belonged, that I was a good leader, and that I could handle anything that was thrown my way.
>
> As the meeting began an issue came up where I found myself in disagreement with the majority of the people on that committee. Instead of listening some more and learning about the people around me, I went off in a self-righteous, arrogant, and disparaging tirade. It did not go well.
>
> At first I felt proud that I had "held my ground." Soon though I knew that something was not right.
>
> The next morning one of the people in that meeting called me to talk. He sat down in my office and after listening carefully, he lovingly called me to repentance. I was amazed when, after contacting all the members of the committee, I was granted forgiveness. We could begin again and we did!
>
> —Juan Huertas
> Pastor, Grace Community United Methodist Church, Shreveport, LA

Ericsson, a research psychologist who has studied the science of expertise.

Ericsson believes in the importance of "deliberate practice," which means that in order to get better at something, we must put in the time and practice that skill in a targeted area, including receiving feedback so that we can improve in that targeted area (as opposed to improving "in general"). Deliberate practice also entails going out of your comfort zone because you're learning new skills, which can mean failure. Dubner and Ericsson discussed one of the barriers to engaging in deliberate practice in people's careers (in addition to not wanting to experience discomfort!): the assumption that they already know all they need to know.

DUBNER: There's a scary part of your book that is about how many people in many professions, as they do it longer, they get more experienced, and there's an assumption that they're getting better and better. But you write that, "Once a person reaches that level of 'acceptable performance and automaticity,' the additional years of 'practice' don't lead to improvement."

ERICSSON: I think this points out that difference between deliberate practice and experience. If you're just doing the same thing over and over, you're not going to prepare yourself for dealing with a complicated situation.[1]

When I listened to this podcast, that phrase—"acceptable performance and automaticity"—stuck with me. So many of us fall into the lull of "acceptable performance and automaticity" in the church, doing the same thing over and over. That's what Dubner means by "practice," as opposed to "deliberate practice." Why should I deliberately practice something that I've already got a degree in or that I've done for years? It's much easier to fall into a routine where competency becomes our trusted companion and we don't have to stretch or risk or fail.

Because we live in an ever-changing society that isn't begging for more churches, however, failing to risk and experience smaller failures means larger failures are looming for churches and denominations.

"As we enter into the postmodern era in the twenty-first century, we can no longer keep doing what worked in the modern era twentieth-century church," said Beth Ann Estock, a co-author of the book, *Weird Church*, and a consultant with the Epicenter Group, an organization that has coached more than a thousand churches in North America and Europe. "If the church does not keep pace with our fast-changing world through experimentation, risk, and failure, we will continue to decline, growing more irrelevant at a time when the planet needs us the most. This requires a contemplative practice of opening our hearts, letting go of our need to control outcomes, and listening deeply to our contexts and community for where Christ is already showing up."[2]

The message of Jesus is as timely and relevant as ever. Your neighbors' need to know about this message hasn't changed, but their lifestyles and ways of receiving information and inspiration has. One way to "immunize" our churches from larger failures (like the closing of a ministry) is by "inoculating" them with the risks and failures that come with actually engaging our communities. Knocking on doors. Asking for sit-down conversations with local leaders. Walking in parades. Being a bold presence on social media. Not all of these efforts will be successful, but they put churches on the road to long-term and robust health.

As I think about a systematized way of integrating failure into your ministry, I suggest that five key components should be present:

1. Pray for courageous hearts
2. Think different
3. Set failure goals
4. Know the importance of not being earnest
5. Do a review

Pray for Courageous Hearts

Can I confess something here about prayer? I sometimes don't pay much attention to it. I don't mean to say I'm anti-prayer. I've developed a routine over the past twenty-five-plus years in which I regularly utilize spiritual disciplines like contemplation, imagination, journaling, and silence as foundations to my day. That's not what I'm talking about. I'm talking about when I used to read about a new ministry initiative that listed all the nuts and bolts needed for success. My eyes would immediately go to the nuts and bolts, the tangible things that I could use to act right away: how much money, how many people, what kind of supplies, how long a timeline, etc.

Often somewhere on one of these lists, prayer was also mentioned. It might be first. It might be last. But it's there, and my eyes would sometimes skim over that part. I may have remembered to offer a prayer before engaging in this ministry, but sometimes, I confess, I didn't. Maybe I'm wrong, but I don't think this attitude toward prayer is terribly abnormal in the mainline church. We spiritual leaders mean well and we ask for prayer, but I'm not sure how intentional we are about it. But church planting has changed me, which is why I list "praying for courageous hearts" first on this list.

About a month before Trey and I submitted our proposal to our bishop to plant a multi-site church in the city, we did a church-planting pilgrimage of sorts to Orlando to attend a conference called Exponential, which I now know is one of the most influential annual gatherings for church planters in the country. Those few days were unbelievably influential. Trey and I certainly learned a lot, and it gave us a chance to deepen our relationship, which was vital for the ups and downs of church planting that we were to experience. This was also the place where I heard over and over the necessity of having a team of people intentionally praying for your new church.

I realize what I'm saying here is nothing new. I'd heard this same message countless times from countless church leaders, but, as I noted earlier, I would give this wisdom a cursory nod as if to say, I hear you, but then I really wouldn't follow through as seriously as I could or should have. So if you're like I used to be and are tempted to just skip to the next step, I'm asking you to stop. Don't. I'm not saying that if you get a certain number of people praying for something, then you'll have magic results, but I am saying that Trey and I heard the counsel to take prayer seriously and we took it to heart. It was immensely helpful.

When we made the announcement about this new church we were starting, we asked people for their prayers, but we also were very intentional in asking a few people to covenant to pray daily for us and this new venture. We thought carefully about whom to ask. We wanted to make sure that once people said yes to this commitment to pray for us daily, they would do their best to follow through. In turn, we sent weekly emails giving them updates on the church and told them how they could continue to pray for us. I can't recall if I specifically asked for this, but I'm pretty sure I was thinking that one of the things they could pray for was that we could live into Psalm 31:24: "Be strong, and let your heart take courage, all you who wait for the Lord." I knew that having a courageous heart would be vital.

We spent our first summer engaging in numerous one-on-one meetings with individuals in the city to share about our new venture, but also to hear stories of the city and its citizens' deeply felt needs. One of the first meetings I had that summer was with a retired United Church of Christ pastor. As we sat in that coffee shop and I explained our vision to him, I'll never forget one of the things he said to me: "Don't be afraid to be big. Too few churches in the mainline are afraid of having a big impact." That comment stuck with me, and so we allowed ourselves to do just that. Dream big.

This pastor's comment both affirmed our willingness to be audacious, but it also made us realize that having a big impact is something we simply couldn't do alone. Thinking about having a big impact made real a piece of Scripture that I'd always liked but which had never fully become part of me: "Now to [God] who by the power at work within us is able to accomplish abundantly far more than all we can ask or imagine . . ." (Ephesians 3:20). I had always been drawn to the "accomplish abundantly" part. Who doesn't want abundant accomplishments? But I sometimes forgot the first part, that there is a Source of power at work within us. That comes first, before any kind of accomplishments can be realized.

Deciding to integrate failure into your ministry takes an inordinate amount of courage, a kind of courage that none of us can muster on our own. Integrating failure means you will be taking new risks and setting yourself up for potential ridicule. I don't know about you, but risk and ridicule aren't things I can handle on my own. I can only take these first steps because of the courageous heart that others have intentionally prayed into me.

Please don't skip this first step. Please don't give it a friendly wave and quickly move to the nuts and bolts. Taking risks that can end in failure is very hard. Truly, the only way you'll make it through is if you're intentional about having others pray for a courageous heart for you—and by praying for it yourself.

Think Different

I know, I know, I'm totally ripping off Apple here, but I recently read Walter Isaacson's biography of Steve Jobs (a great book on failure, by the way), and the technology company's famous "Think different" campaign that ran in the late 1990s and early 2000s has had a new impact on me.

I used to be like many others who were confused by the incorrect grammar of the "Think different" campaign. Shouldn't it be "Think differently"? If "different" is a modifier, then "different" should be an adverb, and the appropriate "ly" should be added.

(Yes, I'm still trying to impress all my former English teachers.) But modifying "different" isn't what Jobs had in mind. According to the Jacobson's biography, "Jobs insisted that he wanted 'different' to be used as a noun, as in 'think victory' or 'think beauty.' Jobs also specifically said that 'think differently' wouldn't have the same meaning to him. Also, Jobs wanted to make it sound colloquial, like the phrase 'think big.' "[3]

I see where Jobs was coming from. There's a significant difference between thinking differently and thinking different. I believe the church has tried to think differently, and it needs to start thinking different. Adding contemporary music to worship and projecting lyrics onto a screen is thinking differently. Moving from a paper newsletter to an electronic one is thinking differently. Preaching a topical sermon series instead of following the lectionary is thinking differently. There's nothing wrong with doing any of these things. I've done them. I continue to do them. But thinking differently doesn't necessarily entail a big risk, and then you probably won't fail at anything. The church needs to do more than think differently. It needs to think different. It needs ministries like Simple Church.

I'm guessing if you made a list of top clergy "small" failures (e.g. forgetting the groom's name at a wedding), acquiring past-their-prime chickens (the live kind, not the kind that you'd serve at a pot luck) wouldn't make that list. Meet Zach Kerzee, part-time baker, part-time egg gatherer, part-time door knocker. All of these job descriptions (and more) add up to him being the full-time pastor of Simple Church, a new United Methodist Church in North Grafton, Massachusetts, which Zach started in July 2014. Zach and the folks at Simple Church definitely think (and act) different.

Zach graduated from Harvard Divinity School in 2014 and was invited by the New England Annual Conference to come to North Grafton to start a new church. Zach had a vision for the kind of church he wanted to start: owning no building, focusing on eating together, leaving a small environmental footprint, and engaging in thoughtful and robust conversations. Simple.

There had been a UMC in North Grafton, but it closed in 2011, and the conference still owned the parsonage. Zach and his wife moved in, and he started building relationships one neighbor at a time. In these days of trying to reach people through great search engine optimization and high click-through rates, Zach also did things simply, knocking on doors and introducing himself as the new United Methodist pastor in town. He got his pitch down to twenty seconds, and it worked. Some of the folks Zach met by going door-to-door started gathering together on Thursday nights for dinner church (more about that in a second) two months after he started introducing himself to his neighbors.

How does Simple Church think different? Here are just a couple of ways:

- Instead of feeling pressure to get involved in church activities several days a week, participants at Simple Church deepen their faith in multiple ways when they gather on Thursday nights. They serve because folks come early to get ready for the meal and stay after to help clean up. They worship by singing simple songs that individuals from the congregation often write themselves. They engage in Bible study because Zach doesn't preach a traditional sermon. He gives them a four-minute "sermon starter" (kind of like what yeast does for bread, he says) and then the people reflect, laugh, argue, and question for the next thirty minutes about the text.

- Simple Church receives most of its revenue not from financial offerings, but from an idea that came about when they served the Eucharist. They had been baking their own bread for communion, and a couple of people suggested to Zach that they should sell the bread to earn a little extra money. It wasn't wildly successful at first. Zach said they went to an off-the-beaten-path general store and struggled to sell a few loaves. But they found their niche at farmer's markets, and the bread-selling business took off. Now they have a whole system in place. The congregation has a full-time baker on staff and sets a goal of selling three hundred loaves per week at numerous farmer's markets (Zach creatively calls this "unawkward evangelism") and using a community-supported agriculture (CSA) model through which individuals give money and then have bread delivered to their homes. Zach's goal is not to do away with Simple Church members contributing financially, but, if everything goes to plan, the church will support itself with the bread revenue and then offerings will go to non-profits in the North Grafton area.

Starting the church has not been without its failures, of course. Soon after they started meeting on Thursday nights, Zach was hearing that some folks had a desire to meet on Friday nights, so he quickly decided to have two weekly gatherings. They started in the second half of December, but were soon hit with a snowstorm that would be a harbinger of a historically severe winter. The momentum for a second night never got going.

"Oh, the Friday night thing failed so bad," Zach said. "I was really enthusiastic about the second night, and I thought I was this super church planter by expanding so quickly. We started off with twenty-five, but then it went to ten and then five, and the snow kept piling up so we decided to pull the plug pretty quickly. It would have been prideful for me to keep going."[4]

That failure hasn't stopped Zach from thinking different, though, and he still hopes to expand. He currently has about sixty people in the Simple Church orbit and thirty-five to forty gather on a typical Thursday night. They're also expanding their food offerings to include eggs. The parsonage is located on a working farm, and so in addition to spending time baking bread, Zach gathers eggs from fifteen chickens every day. That's the reason for the aforementioned failure of acquiring older chickens. Zach bought four chickens at first, but they were only producing two eggs per week. Zach learned: acquire younger chickens and more of them. The things you learn when you fail in creative ministry!

Zach and the folks at Simple Church get it. They think different, and they do it with energy and a passionate desire to share the gospel in all kinds of contexts, recognizing that failure is not only inevitable, but something to be celebrated. If you want more examples of ministries that are thinking different, I highly recommend *Weird Church*, which I quoted earlier. The authors share many stories of churches that are trying different things in different contexts.

As you contemplate thinking differently about church, then, consider dropping that "ly" and going from adverb to noun.

Set Failure Goals

Imagine you're standing on a street corner on a rainy day. The weather forecast said mostly sunny when you walked out of your home that morning, so you didn't bring your umbrella, but the clouds moved in quickly, and now it's raining. You're getting soaked as you fervently look around for a cab, though none can be found. While this is certainly frustrating, there's a part of you that isn't surprised. It's a rainy day, you reason, so more people are hailing cabs, which makes finding a cab more difficult. Isn't that the logic?

You would think so, but a study done in 1997 about New York City taxi drivers told a different story. The study found that there is more than one reason why you're getting soaked on that street corner. Cab drivers may have already met their daily quota, and so they took the rest of the day off, which decreases the number of available cabs. Drivers were given a goal to make a certain amount of money per day. On rainy days, many drivers hit their goal early and then felt little incentive to stay out on the streets and, say, give a ride to a person standing on a corner getting soaked, like yourself in this scenario. This research is an example of what can happen when goals are set with an inappropriate time frame.

This is just one example of "goals gone wild," which is the title of a working paper published by the Harvard Business School in 2009. The authors of the paper warn that systematic harm caused by goal setting has been largely ignored. Goals go wild because individuals are sometimes so focused on meeting a goal that harmful side effects occur, such as "a narrow focus that neglects non-goal areas, a rise in unethical behavior, distorted risk preferences, corrosion of organizational culture, and reduced intrinsic motivation."[5]

We live in a goal-saturated culture, and churches are not immune to this. "Benchmarking" is a key word used in church planting to make sure that planters are raising enough money, getting enough people in worship, and meeting with enough people. The authors state that there's nothing inherently wrong with goal setting, but the process must be done carefully. The paper points to another study that cites Steve Kerr, an executive at General Electric and an expert in reward and punishment. Kerr advises managers "to avoid setting goals that increase employee stress, to refrain from punishing failure, and to provide the tools employees need to meet ambitious goals."[6] The use of the word "failure" here, of course, caught my attention and made me wonder, what if failing *were a goal in and of itself?*

Let me stress again that accountability and setting goals by traditional church measurement standards (e.g. worship attendance, financial giving) are not bad things. But I fear that too often these benchmarks do just the things that Kerr says should be avoided: they increase stress and punish failure. Setting realistic goals, then, is one way to respond to this line of thinking. But what if goal setting was taken a step farther and in a different direction? How great would it be if a denominational official also said, "I want you to fail at least three times this week" or "I want you to risk starting at least one new ministry this year that will not go as well as you'd like" and then insisted that the failure not only be measured, but celebrated?

We can learn from new ventures that tank. But I don't think I've ever experienced or heard someone talk about a time when folks said, "We really missed the boat on that one, and now we have better understanding. Let's give ourselves a hand for this failure!" I'll confess that we're still working on this at Urban Village. We haven't gotten too specific yet, but I do hope that we can risk at least three ventures this year that will not turn out the way we wanted.

If planning to fail seems too challenging or too out-of-the-box for you, at the very least begin celebrating failures when they do arise. I'll talk more about Brené Brown in my next chapter, but in her book *Rising Strong,* she highlights the organization Engineers Without Borders Canada (EWB). Normally organizations try to sweep their failures under the rug, but in an attempt to bring failure into the (lime)light, EWB has published its failures in a special annual report every year since 2008. They explain why on their website:

EWB believes that success in development is not possible without taking risks and innovating—which inevitably means failing sometimes. We also believe that it's important to publicly celebrate these failures, which allows us to share the lessons more broadly and create a culture that encourages creativity and calculated risk taking. This is a culture we value within EWB.[7]

This is just one example of how more individuals and organizations are not hiding from their failures but celebrating them.

Celebrating failures after risking something may be easier than actually setting failure goals, but however you do it, you must account for failure and expect it. If you try something new and nothing bad happens, you may have set the bar so low that success was inevitable. Plan for failure. Celebrate it. And then you can learn from it.

The Importance of Not Being Earnest

I know some companies and organizations have a famous cocktail-napkin story, wherein the founders of said company/organization were sitting at some drinking establishment (be it coffee or alcohol), came up with the idea, and grabbed a cocktail napkin to draw out the germ of a plan. It's a great story to have and even better if you have the actual napkin.

I don't think Trey or I drew on a napkin. We probably scribbled on regular old paper (and it was probably Trey who scribbled, as he tended to do more of that than I did). But when we first started talking about the idea of planting a church together at a Corner Bakery on the corner of Washington and Wells, I'll never forget one of the things Trey said that I'm sure must have been written down on that piece of paper. I'm paraphrasing here, but I remember Trey saying something like, "So many churches today are so *earnest*. I want us to have fun while we're doing this." You may know that the mission of Google is, "Don't be evil"; one of the unofficial mottoes I've always had about our church is, "Don't be earnest."

That's not to say we don't take our work and ministry seriously. We do. But when seriousness and earnestness dominate an organization's culture, these attributes can heighten the negative impact of failure. I fear it's one of the side effects of the sky-is-falling mentality of some mainline church leaders. Decline begets fear, which begets earnestness, which ramps up the anxiety whenever one tries something new.

One of the programs that churches have tried over the past few years to reverse decline is Natural Church Development (NCD), a system that promotes church health by identifying eight core areas (or "quality characteristics") and encouraging churches to focus on its minimum factor, or the weakest of the areas. By becoming healthy in these areas, the authors of NCD believe, a church will naturally grow. I used NCD at the two churches I pastored before starting Urban Village, and I found it to be a helpful tool. Something that always struck me about NCD, though, was one of its findings about laughter.

One of those quality characteristics that NCD says is necessary is called Loving Relationships, which, of course, makes sense. It would be hard to fathom a healthy church that didn't promote and exemplify loving relationships. But the book shared an interesting finding: "The question of whether there is much laughter in a church has a strong correlation to the quality of a church and its growth. Interestingly enough, aspects like this find little mention in church growth literature."[8] According to NCD surveys, 68 percent of people in "high quality, growing" churches agreed with the statement, "There is a lot of laughter in our church," compared to 33 percent in "low quality, declining" churches.

Now, I'm not suggesting that we replace open communion tables with open mic nights for comedians (though that is an intriguing idea), but I do think there's something to be said for having a certain lightness when trying new things that will likely fail.

Sometimes laughing is the only thing we can do when we consider the ways God is moving in our midst. I love the way Genesis describes Abraham when he first hears the news from God that he and his wife Sarai will have a son: "Then Abraham fell on his face and laughed, and said to himself, 'Can a child be born to a man who is a hundred years old? Can Sarah, who is ninety years old, bear a child?'" (Gen. 17:17). Earlier in chapter 17, Abraham fell on his face as a way to venerate God. Here in verse 17, Abraham falls on his face in laughter. Was it the kind of laugh one emits after hearing a joke? Was it a nervous laugh, because Abraham's pent-up emotion has to come out somehow? (I remember going on roller coasters as a kid with my dad, and instead of screaming when going down a huge hill, my dad would laugh, I think because he had to somehow express the fear and excitement he was feeling. Laughter was a natural response.) Maybe the vision that God was putting before Abraham was so weighty and awesome that he had to acknowledge the ridiculousness of what he was hearing by laughing.

In his book *Between Heaven and Mirth: Why Joy, Laughter, and Humor Are at the Center of the Spiritual Life,* James Martin reminds readers of Jesus' sense of humor. He believes, for example, that at the beginning of the Gospel of John when Nathaniel hears about Jesus as this alleged Messiah and that Jesus is from Nazareth, he cracks a joke. "Can anything good come out of Nazareth?" Martin believes that Jesus gets the joke by responding, "Here is truly an Israelite in whom there is no deceit!" Martin continues:

When I imagine Jesus, it is not simply as a person who heals the sick, raises the dead, stills the storm and preaches the good news. It's also as a man of great good-will and compassion, with a zest for life, someone unafraid of controversy, free to be who he knows himself to be and brimming with generous good humor. Full of high spirits. Playful. Even fun.[9]

Playful? Fun? When was the last time you heard these adjectives used when describing a ministry initiative? And yet when we begin thinking different about church, I believe these adjectives are necessities, especially when we know that failure will probably accompany these initiatives. Some organizations get this.

My family went on a summer road trip a few years ago to visit my wife's brother and his family in New Hampshire. One of our stops on the way home was the Ben & Jerry's factory in Waterbury, Vermont. Ice cream is my dessert of choice, so you'll usually find that our freezer is fairly well stocked with Ben & Jerry's (Americone Dream being my latest favorite). My wife and I had been to the factory once many years ago before, so it was fun to bring our kids along this time. In addition to taking the tour, seeing where the ice cream is made, and getting our free tastes afterward, we wandered around the grounds for a while. We were enjoying the warm June afternoon when we stumbled onto a graveyard. Well, not just any graveyard, but a Flavor Graveyard.

The Ben & Jerry's website says it best: "Ben & Jerry's is known for outrageous, chunky, funky flavors. But outrageous flavor experimentation comes with some risks, and flavors can meet their untimely end even without using a spoon. That's okay with us, because ice cream flavors, like everything else, have a beginning and an end."[10] The graveyard (which you can also view online) contains about thirty-five flavors that have been tried and failed over the years.

I love this graveyard concept, and I think churches can learn a thing or two from it. First, they haven't hidden the fact that they've introduced some less-than-popular flavors. Ever heard of the flavors Fossil Fuel? Oh Pear? Coconutterly Fair? Probably not. They were on the shelves for just a brief time, and I'm sure it must have been tempting for executives to hide the fact that these flavors tanked, but they live on in the Flavor Graveyard. As the company notes on its website in a section about experimentation, the graveyard conveys a message that they will continue to try new things, and they'll continue to not get it right. (Memo to Ben & Jerry's: any ice cream with coconut in it—see Coconutterly Fair— deserves a burial.)

Second, they treat these failures with levity. Each of the deceased flavors gets its own tombstone in the graveyard, and each has a humorous epitaph. Here's the one for Wavy Gravy:

Just so there's no confusion, we thought we oughtta warn
   ya:
Wavy Gravy isn't dead—he lives in California.
No such luck for Wavy's flavor, but we've been wrong
   before,
We won't give up the ghost if you won't, so what're you
   waiting for?

And not only do they provide tombstones, they also have actual funerals when they retire/end a flavor and offer tongue-in-cheek articles on their website, with titles like, "The Five Stages of Flavor Grief: What to do When Your Favorite Flavor is Retired to the Flavor Graveyard."

Ben & Jerry's gets it. Now, you might think, "Well, that's ice cream. We're doing something much more serious. We're dealing with peoples' *souls*." Perhaps. We should take our ministries seriously, and some people may feel that, for example, a mock funeral for a church program that went awry dishonors those who put a lot of time and effort into it. But I fear that seriousness has overtaken all aspects of the church life these days to the point where we actually start believing the church's success hinges on what *we* do. When that happens, the only one who's laughing is probably God.

Do a Review

Put Johnny Depp, Julianne Moore, and Reese Witherspoon together, and you've got the makings of a Hollywood blockbuster, but that's not why I've combined them. These actors all have something in common. They dislike watching themselves on screen. In an interview in 2010, Witherspoon said this: "No, I can't watch myself. I don't know. Who feels good looking at themselves. . . ? Nobody, right? And it's torture! Why would you want to watch yourself being stupid and pretending to be someone else?"[11]

Why would you want to watch yourself being stupid, indeed? It's one of the toughest things about learning from your failures. I usually say the Ignatian prayer of *examen* every night and, even to this day, the hardest night for me is Sunday because, as I reflect on the day, I reflect on worship and my sermon, and that sometimes sends me into a state of discouragement. Why did I use that illustration? Why did we sing that song? Many of us can be our own worst critics, and when we're forced to look at things that nobody thought went well, that's even worse. And yet doing a review of our failures is necessary.

Before I talk about the process of learning from one's failures, I want to acknowledge that there's a very important step that I'm

I remember feeling lost and unsure what was going on. I kept flipping pages and somehow not seeing what everybody else was talking about. It seemed like everybody had a clue around the table except for me. Then it dawned on me. I was the only one who couldn't read and understand the expense report, let alone the columns in the Excel spreadsheet. I felt embarrassed and grossly unprepared for the pastoral role I had embarked upon. Seminary had prepared me to preach, order the church in polity, serve my community, and share in the sacraments. But nobody ever mentioned that I would need to know anything about finances, human resources, building maintenance, and capital campaigns.

After my initial finance meeting, I made a vow to myself not only to trust people in servant leadership positions who had calling, capacity, character, chemistry, and competency but also to educate myself with the knowledge of what was taking place in the life of the church when it comes to the natural: space, systems, structures, and $$$. It was time to have discussion with colleagues from the business world, to read pertinent articles, to start watching trends regarding the economy, and to pay close attention to what was coming into and going out from my local church.

—Rosario Picardo
Executive Pastor, New Church Development
Ginghamsburg Church, Ginghamsburg, OH

skipping for now: Allowing yourself to name and sit with the pain of failure. This is important. It's so important, in fact, that I'm devoting chapter 5 to the topic. In her book *Rising Strong,* Brené Brown notes that embracing failure without acknowledging hurt is "gold-plating grit. To strip failure of its real emotional consequences is to scrub the concepts of grit and resilience of the very qualities that make them both so importance—toughness, doggedness, and perseverance."[12] So we'll get to dealing with the pain later.

For now, we want to make sure that we are *learning* from failure, so we don't simply fail for failure's sake. This isn't easy, of course, because who, other than coroners, likes to do autopsies? Evaluation is crucial, though. When people ask us about church planting and whether there are particular conferences to attend or books to read, we often encourage them to think about going through community organizing training, which, among other things, helps individuals learn the necessity of building public relationships. Something else we've learned from community organizing is that anything worth doing is worth evaluating.

We haven't perfected the art of evaluation at Urban Village, but we have learned it's almost impossible to be totally objective about evaluation. Real people put in lots of real hours, and they understandably have ownership in what they created and how it turned out. That's why you can't forget the tried-and-true process of naming the things that went well and honoring the faithful effort. There's an emotional aspect to risking and failing, which is why it's key to remember some of the things I've already mentioned: the importance of not being earnest, the importance of naming and acknowledging the pain of failing, and the truth that your true identity is not failure but belovedness.

But you also have to speak the truth in love (with others and with yourself) when evaluating, and there are practical steps you can follow. First, you have to be intentional about including evaluation in your ministry plan. People put a lot of time into planning or organizing an event, and the vast majority of their efforts understandably go into the steps leading up to the event. You may have people on your team who love to plan, love to put the steps down so that we know that we need to do four weeks out from the event, three weeks out, etc. These folks are invaluable, and since planning is not a huge strength of mine, I always am unbelievably grateful when these gifted individuals are on my team. In my experience, though, even the best planners sometimes fail to include a post-event meeting where you evaluate what happened. Often (and I definitely include myself in this), you're so unbelievably relieved and exhausted when the event is over that you want to just put all your notes in a file folder or an Internet cloud to maybe review in the future. But later evaluation rarely happens. When you plan something, then, you have to make sure that you also include a post-event gathering. Make it a celebration of both the lives you touched *and* the failures that occurred.

Second, as you go about working the plan or creating the event, make sure someone is recording everything, and make sure that you know where this information is, especially if the event is annual. There have been times at Urban Village when we've done the evaluation after the event and identified some good things to do differently the next time, and somebody writes notes and puts them into some Internet cloud, and the event comes along the next year and we forget: (a) who recorded the notes and (b) where the notes are, which means (c) we are relying on our memories. The tricky thing about memories, though, is they become hazy, and we tend to remember all the wonderful things that happened and never remember the failures.

People often want to know about the beginnings of Urban Village and how it all started. As we get farther away from the summer of 2009, my memory is already transforming those first few months. I forget how really hard they were and instead blissfully talk about the mere challenges that we effortlessly hurdled. I look back at those early times with rose-colored glasses, as we all do. That is, until I read some of my journal entries. Here's an entry from July 17, 2009, less than three weeks after we started: "I know it's only been a couple weeks, but it would be great to see just a tiny bit of fruit or at least some call-backs from potential members. Had a hard time sleeping last night, feeling a little stressed already. Not sure I could do this by myself." Or this one from August 5, 2009: "I'd really like to see *something*. A tiny miracle. A coincidence. Some spark of interest from someone. Answer me when I call, O God! God is with me. My call is to be faithful and *not give up*. Help me glorify you, Lord. All I can do is be faithful. But I'd still like a miracle." One more, Sept. 24, 2009: "Just a few days ago, I loved this gig. Now, it sucks. No one gets back to me and these meetings don't go anywhere. I'd like to see a little fruit!!"

I mention all of this to emphasize that we cannot simply rely on our memories. We must document failures and then actually use what we learn when we attempt these events and programs again. One of the nice things about writing this book is that I'm able to document something we recently tried, so one hopes there's no way we'll forget!

The site that I oversee at Urban Village recently moved back to the South Loop neighborhood, which is where we started. (I'll say more about this move in the next chapter.) One of the many ways we've been publicizing our return is by giving away coffee to strangers on the street. We ordered coffee-cup sleeves, stamped the UVC logo on them, negotiated a great price with a local coffee shop (as we would also be publicizing their coffee), and then set out to give away coffee during the morning commute.

We weren't quite sure about a few things, though. For example, when was the best time to give the coffee away? What would be the best location? Should we devise a coffee distribution system, so that we handed the coffee out efficiently? We started by giving it away in front of one of the many high-rises in the neighborhood. Figuring out an effective way to do outreach in high-rises has been one of the more challenging evangelism puzzles for us, so we figured giving away coffee in front of the entrance would be a good start. We also decided to begin at 7:00 a.m. We quickly realized that we weren't getting much foot traffic at that location, so we tried another corner that was a bit busier but still left us worried that we were going to have a lot of unused coffee. We finally went closer to one of the train stations, a move which was more successful. We didn't have a great system of pouring the coffee, getting cream and sugar ready if a person wanted it, and handing out information about the coffee shop and our church.

After we finally got rid of the coffee (which took longer and was harder than we thought it would be), we took some time to evaluate the morning to see where improvements could be made. It was pretty easy to point out the failures. First, we started at the wrong location. Second, we started too early. People don't really get out and about in this particular area until 7:30 at the earliest. Third, we realized that Friday may not have been the best day to do this. We had conversations with other commuters and learned that, more and more in the corporate world, people work from home on Fridays. Finally, we needed a more organized and uniform system of offering the coffee, and we wondered whether wearing a uniform of sorts (like the same stocking cap) would legitimize what we were doing.

So we tried again. We did another coffee giveaway a couple weeks later and started at a later time (7:45) on a Thursday at the train station. The evangelism chair of our Wicker Park site volunteered to provide aprons and hand-painted the Urban Village logo on them. We had coffee ready to hand out and eager volunteers walked among commuters, offering the cups with UVC sleeves. It may have made a difference that it was about twenty degrees colder the second time we tried it, but the first time we attempted the coffee giveaway, it took us ninety minutes to go through three boxes of coffee. The second time took us only twenty minutes, and the volunteers would have gone back to order more coffee if their teeth weren't chattering from the cold!

We were intentional about post-event evaluating and recording what went well and what didn't. The only thing we weren't intentional about was somehow celebrating the "failures" of the first effort. This is a lesson that's clearly still hard for me to learn; we did the coffee giveaway while I was working on this book! I still went into the first coffee giveaway determined that we were going to nail this process right off the bat, with no flaws or messups. I should have planned for failure and then, when it happened, found a way to commend ourselves for trying something new rather than just asking, what can we learn from this?

Reese Witherspoon is right. It's painful to watch yourself being stupid. But pain is better than a slow death, which can happen when we don't evaluate and learn from our failures.

Trypanophobia is the fear of needles, and many of us probably self-diagnose as having this phobia. The next time I hear someone say, "I can't wait to go in for my flu shot!" will be the first. But going through this discomfort is often necessary to stave off something much more serious in the future.

No one starts a ministry and says, "I can't wait to see what failures come out of this!" I know I don't. I still get anxious and worry about how I'll be perceived if this new thing doesn't work out. But taking chances and stubbing our toes is necessary, so that something more serious doesn't happen to our church in the future.

5

LIVING WITH THE PAIN OF FAILURE

You've no doubt noticed by now that interspersed throughout this book are numerous stories shared by church leaders about moments when they have failed. I was slightly apprehensive when approaching colleagues because, well, it's not the easiest email to write when you essentially say, "I'm writing a book about failure and I want you in it!" I assured them that I didn't think *they* were failures, but when I explained the concept of the book, they were all more than willing. In fact, the most common response I received was, "You only want one?"

Rachel Gilmore (whose story is found on page 28) is a great example. I wrote and invited her to submit a 150-word story. Less than twenty-four hours later, she sent me five stories totaling more a thousand words. She described the time she hosted an art show depicting victims of human trafficking and no one showed up; the time she and her leaders didn't secure the trailer that held all their Sunday morning "stuff" (music stands, Bibles, nursery toys, etc.) and someone drove off with it; the time she didn't train her small-group leaders properly after experiencing growth in discipleship and then had one group resemble something out of the *Lord of the Flies*; the time she was so into church planting that she advertised her son's first birthday on Meetup.com and so had a houseful of strangers roaming around her home for the party—that was a moment when she realized that she was sacrificing her family for her ministry. And, of course, she included the story you read here in this book. When Rachel sent me her stories, the first line in her email read, "Is it bad that I have a lot of failure examples that come to mind?"

Like bubble gum (or worse) sticking to the bottom of our shoes, the memories of our failures remain in our minds far longer than we may want them to. We may work hard at scrubbing those stories out of our consciousness because it just hurts too much. But sitting with those stories—rather than erasing them—may be the best thing we can do.

As I mentioned in the last chapter, people sometimes go from failing at something to fixing what's "broken" with little acknowledgment of the fact that failing doesn't feel good. There are countless stories of people who triumph after experiencing adversity, and we tend to dwell on the triumph part and not so much on how painful the adversity was (and is). Maybe we think if we ignore the pain or move quickly through the difficulty, then we can get to the triumph that much faster. But that's not usually how it works. The sting of failure lingers and reminds us that even though we can try to ignore it or move on quickly from it, it's not going anywhere and could potentially do further damage if we don't deal with it head on.

Before we get into confronting it, though, I think it's important to at least explore why failure hurts in the first place and name the fact that failure can literally be physically painful.

In the December 2000 issue of the *European Journal of Pain* (no, I'm not a subscriber), an article titled "Does Failure Hurt? The Effects of Failure Feedback on Pain Report, Pain Tolerance and Pain Avoidance" found that when individuals are told that they failed at a task, their pain tolerance decreased as compared to individuals who were told that they succeeded.[1]

The authors of the report studied fifty-four female college students in the Netherlands. One group was given an intelligence test that was set up for them to succeed, while another group was given a test that was set up for them to fail, and one control group was given a test that simply measured their own artistic tastes, with no measurement of success or failure. After taking the test, each individual was given the results. Each member of the "failure" group was told that her score was very low in comparison to other students her age. To make matters worse, the official giving the results made several statements emphasizing each student's failure. In contrast, each member of the "success" group was told that her score was very high in comparison to other students her age and was given reinforcing comments.

After receiving the results, each student was then asked to participate in a "cold pressor" test, wherein they stuck their hand into an ice-cold bucket of water and, after thirty-second intervals, were asked to rate the intensity and unpleasantness of the pain. Perhaps not surprisingly, the study found that those in the "failure" group had a lower tolerance for physical pain and discomfort than those in the success group. Failure, then, leads not only to emotional pain, but one could argue opens us up to greater risk of physical pain, too.

The Downside of Comparison

This study gives some scientific grounding to what we may already know. Failure hurts. But that still doesn't answer the question: *Why* does failure hurt? There are different ways to respond to this question. In her book, *Rising Strong*, Brené Brown notes that failure is painful because "it fuels the 'shouldas and couldas,' which means judgment and shame are often lying in wait."[2] In a March 7, 2016, online article in *Forbes*, Bill Fischer writes, "Failure hurts because it is just that, failure! Even when done well, small failure can be costly. If you fail over and over again, you could jeopardize your chances for future success, no matter who you are or how small the cost."[3]

I'm especially interested, however, in how *comparing ourselves to others, particularly our vocational peers,* plays a role in this damage. I mentioned comparison earlier in the book, but I think it bears a closer look.

I think comparison is one of the first tools we use before we succumb to the "deadly" sin of envy. In his book *Envy,* Joseph Epstein describes how we use comparison when we become envious: "You see something, want it, feel it only sensible and right that it belong to you and not the person who has it. Once the injustice of the other person having it is established—this usually doesn't take too long—his unworthiness must be emphasized, at least in your own mind."[4] We see "success" in the ministry of another, whether we know the person or not, and we immediately think of our own ministry and start comparing. That leads us to denigrating the other and, soon enough, ourselves. This is something that both Trey and I freely confessed to each other as we were starting out.

For example, church planting is becoming more and more popular in urban areas and so Urban Village certainly wasn't the only church starting in Chicago in 2009. It was hard not to look at other church plant web sites or hear about growth that they were experiencing and not think bad thoughts about them or find flaws in their theology or ecclesiology. That, in turn, led me to wonder why *we* weren't growing as quickly or what we weren't doing that they were.

We're introduced to envy and comparison pretty early in the Scriptures. You know the story in Genesis 4. Cain, one of the sons of Adam and Eve, brings God an offering of fruit from the ground. His brother Abel brings the Lord an offering of "the firstlings of his flock, their fat portions." We don't know what kind of fruit Cain offered, but clearly Abel brought God his best. We can imagine the comparisons happening even before we read the next verse. Cain looks at Abel's offering, and I can intuit that familiar mixture of anger and low self-worth that must have been coming over him. The Lord's response makes it even worse: "And the Lord had regard for Abel and his offering, but for Cain and his offering he had no regard. So Cain was very angry, and his countenance fell" (Genesis 4:4b-5). Not long after that, of course, Cain invites his brother out for a little stroll and decides to end the pain of comparison and envy by killing the one to whom he was comparing himself.

I think many of us can relate to the feeling of anger and frustration when we're working hard in our ministry and little fruit seems to be forthcoming and then we look at a colleague and it appears to come easily for him or her. Fortunately, instead of taking the severe step of ending the life of the one to whom we're comparing ourselves, we take the alternative route of silently denigrating him or her while slowly harming our own souls.

I believe clergy are particularly prone to the dangers of comparison. As I mentioned in chapter 1, you may compare yourself to a Hero Pastor or to a pastor who serves a congregation in close vicinity to yours—one whose circumstances should presumably produce outcomes similar to those in your congregation. If her church appears to be doing particularly well, the immediate temptation is to compare your church to hers, and if your church isn't showing the kind of life, vitality, and growth in traditional metrics, you feel like a failure. This is particularly tempting in the world of church planting, where it seems like you're benchmarking everything. It even happens with individuals who are on the same ministry team.

Urban Village has received some attention for various reasons, including the fact that it was started by two full-time pastors. Even though there are biblical examples of individuals going out in pairs (e.g., Paul and Barnabas) to start new faith communities, most people are still used to seeing and hearing about pastors doing church plants on their own. It takes a special relationship for a team to work well (even Paul and Barnabas eventually broke up!), which is one of the many reasons why I have been blessed to work with Trey.

When most people think of a church planter, they think of a person who is very outgoing, loves meeting people, connects well, and exudes *something* that will make people want to be a part of a new faith community. In other words, they think of someone like Trey, who is an extrovert extraordinaire. When they meet me (the other founder), I quickly get pegged as the "quiet one." This is not an inaccurate assessment. I tend to be more of an introvert (though not a huge one—I really like a good balance of being by myself and also being with and meeting people), which I think was a reason why I was hesitant to think of myself as a church planter when Trey and I first started dreaming about starting something together. I've since learned that personality type isn't the *only* measure of a church planter. Other things that figure into the success of a new church include a planter's ability to: engage the community rather than spending hours developing the church's

On paper, the plan was perfect: I move to Minneapolis, I plant a multi-ethnic church that focuses on climate change, then this "EcoChurch" movement changes the world.

Well, that was the plan.

I did a focus group with some of my black neighbors, and they told me that "EcoChurch" sounded expensive—like a toilet bowl cleaner that you pay extra for but it cleans just the same. Climate change matters, they said, but unless I first make clear how Black Lives Matter, this ministry is useless.

There goes the perfect plan.

I had to let the vision of "I will plant an EcoChurch" fail. God made clear that *I* wasn't the one who was planting, because only God brings the growth (1 Corinthians 3:6), and this ministry would be better off focusing on environmental justice—with race and class at the forefront. Thank God for well-timed failures!

—Tyler Sit
Church Planter, New City Church, Minneapolis, MN

logo, persevere when setbacks arise, articulate the church's unique mission as it relates to context, talk comfortably about raising money, set boundaries so that the new plant doesn't consume any personal life, and develop a sixth sense about the needs and desires of the neighborhood/town/city. This is not an exhaustive list by any means, and one of the challenges of church planting is that a person can have all of these qualities and a new church still may not flourish. Even though I know all of these things in my head, the notion that all a planter needs is an outgoing personality still lingers in my mind and causes me to occasionally compare myself to any church planter who seems to exude visible charisma and to love the non-stop interaction of others.

I gave some examples in chapter 4 of journal entries I wrote in the first few months of our starting Urban Village. Another entry I recorded (and had completely forgotten about until I went back through my journals for this book) is an example of my comparing myself to Trey. We had organized some sort of gathering, and I noted in my journal that everyone who attended came because of a connection to Trey. "He was responsible for every person in the room," I wrote and underlined for emphasis. I, according to my journal, was responsible for zero people in the room. I could tell by my writing that this fact did little for my confidence, and I know myself well enough to imagine what I must have been thinking: *Maybe Trey should just do this by himself.*

I was comparing my personality to his. I was comparing my "results" with his, and I was coming up short. Yes, I knew (and was affirmed by others) that I had gifts and graces to bring to this new project. Sure, I knew about Paul's metaphor of the body in the book of Romans and reminded myself of that wisdom: "For as in one body we have many members, and not all the members have the same function, so we, who are many, are one body in Christ, and individually we are members one of another. We have gifts that differ according to the grace given to us" (Romans 12:4-6a). But, frankly, that wasn't helpful. Trey's gifts seemed to be so much more *visible,* and the fruits seemed much more *evident,* which made it hard for me to look at my (invisible) gifts and fruits and feel good about them. The temptation to compare and then deem myself a failure was particularly evident in the summer and fall of 2014, and the comparisons extended beyond Trey.

Because being a multi-site church was part of our vision from the beginning and because boldness is one of our core values, we were pretty aggressive about starting other sites quickly after our initial launch in March 2010. I know there are excellent formulas out there that advise churches when it's time to launch a new site, but we measured ourselves more by the calendar than by how many regular worshipers we had (we had about 130, which is normally pretty small for a new church to think about launching another location). Six months after our initial launch in the South Loop (in the general downtown Chicago area), we started our second site, worshiping on Sunday nights in the Wicker Park neighborhood, about five miles northwest of our first location. One year after the Wicker Park site creation, we launched our Andersonville location, about nine miles north of downtown. One year after Andersonville, we relaunched Wicker Park and also began worshiping there on Sunday mornings (our worship numbers had been declining on Sunday nights). And then six months after Wicker Park Launch II, we launched our fourth site about eight miles south of downtown in an area bordering the Hyde Park and Woodlawn neighborhoods. That's five launches in three years, and I feel the need for a nap just remembering all that activity.

To keep up with all the launches, we brought on additional staff, so by the time we launched Hyde Park-Woodlawn, each of the locations had a site pastor. I had settled in at our original site in the South Loop neighborhood. We had first held worship there in a rented theater in the Spertus Institute for Jewish Learning and Leadership on Michigan Avenue. It was a beautiful space with modern architecture and amenities. The rent was a bit out of our price range initially, but we decided to take a risk and make that our first home. We couldn't have asked for a better location. It's centrally located in the city, and folks traveled from around the Chicago area to worship with us.

As we launched additional sites, however, the numbers at the South Loop started to decline. I always knew that Chicago was a city stitched together from neighborhoods, but I have learned how deeply some people feel about where they live and their desire to eat, shop, exercise and, yes, worship within walking distance of their home. It made sense, then, that someone who lives on the north side would want to worship at our Andersonville site, which would also provide an excellent reason for our South Loop attendance numbers to decline.

As much as we loved worshiping at Spertus, then, it became clear that because of the declining numbers, the space was too big and too expensive. We spent some time looking at a couple other locations in the neighborhood, but we were also very conscious (as most churches are) of our budget and our desire to hire a full-time director of discipleship. Because of that, we also looked at surrounding neighborhoods, since rent prices are high in the downtown area. We began a conversation with a United Methodist church about two-and-a-half miles to the north of Spertus that worshiped at 12:30 pm, which meant their sanctuary was empty on Sunday mornings. Would they be interested in letting us worship there? To have strong relationships with other United Methodist churches is one of the blessings of our denomination's connection: they graciously said yes, and we were able to halve the amount of rent we were formerly paying to Spertus. Our time at the church was short-lived, however, and we stayed there only eighteen months.

We had a decent launch at a new location (which we now called River North, a neighborhood in the area) in the spring of 2014, but it didn't take long for me to notice that something wasn't quite right. A few weeks after the launch, our worship attendance numbers were down compared to the year before when we were at Spertus, and we didn't have nearly the same number of visitors. Those things were quantifiable, but I was also sensing something that wasn't easily measurable. We seemed to be lacking energy and life, and I started racking my brain to figure out why. Was it the building? Were people not as attracted to a traditional worship space? Was it the location? Even though we weren't that much farther from Spertus, we were no longer in the middle of what is one of most well-known parts of Chicago—right across the street from Grant Park and within walking distance of all the museums and many restaurants and Lake Michigan. Was it our new worship leader? Our beloved music leader (Sarah), who was with us from the first launch, had resigned before we made the move so she could focus more on her recording career. Our new worship leader was great, but many people had understandably developed a strong attachment to Sarah and missed her.

I mentioned the need in the last chapter for teams to do a review after experiencing failure, and I've given a lot of thought to what we could have done differently with this site move. One of my first mistakes was assuming that everyone who attended our South Loop site would make the move and start attending at our new location. It was only two and a half miles, I thought. It's not *that* far. But remember what I said about Chicago being a city of neighborhoods? Many people did move with us, but I started receiving a few gracious emails from individuals who said, while they appreciated Urban Village, they really wanted to worship at a church in the South Loop, where they lived, shopped, and played. This was one of my many lessons from this "failure": Don't underestimate the power of location when you plant in the city. We do not live in an age where we can assume that people will have undying loyalty to a church. Convenience also plays a factor, because it's not always as easy to hop in a car and find parking in the city as it is in the suburbs.

Another mistake we made was having too much confidence in the reach of the Urban Village brand. We were receiving some notoriety about being a church that expanded so quickly, and this applause started to go to my head a bit. We did some outreach into the new neighborhood but not nearly as much as we did when we launched (or relaunched) our other sites. I figured because Urban Village had name recognition and a solid presence on the Internet, we didn't need to immerse ourselves as intensely into River North. Another lesson: Just because you have some recognition (like Urban Village or The United Methodist Church do), the vast majority of people have never heard of you. No matter what ministry you create, nothing replaces the hard but good work of relationship building with your new neighbors and the nitty-gritty of on-the-street evangelism (like putting up flyers, sidewalk chalking, etc.). Trey has been fond of gently criticizing the oft-cited quotation attributed to St. Francis of Assisi: "Preach the gospel at all times; when necessary, use words." Christians, he fears (and I agree), have used this quote as a cover for avoiding conversations (and evangelism) altogether. Sometimes, you actually need words.

In addition to asking all of these questions when doing the review, though, I asked myself, is the decline because of something I'm doing or not doing? Is it me?

Those last two questions were the ones I wrestled with all summer. They can be good questions to ask, but this kind of self-recrimination also can get out of control, because one loses a sense of perspective. I forgot that I do have gifts and graces, and I started blaming everything on myself. What made matters worse for me emotionally was that two of the other sites' worship attendance numbers were increasing steadily. And this is where the comparison thing got ugly.

For a time during our weekly staff meetings, we would check in, site by site, and report how things went the previous Sunday, and sometimes we'd share worship attendance numbers. This is a natural and understandable thing to do, but I grew to resent this check-in. It got to the point where I *would be happy when the other sites had low attendance.* How crazy is that? I loved the people I worked with. They were (and are) friends, but when they would celebrate their site's growth and when my site declined, those comparisons drove me further into self-doubt and self-criticism. *What am I doing wrong? Why am I failing?* And the question would pop up again that popped up the first summer when we started Urban Village: Would it be better if Trey were the sole leader of this whole thing?

That's what was on my mind when I had breakfast with Trey later that summer. He and I checked in every other week, and it was over pancakes that morning that I told him I seriously doubted how much longer I could go on like this. I told him that I was tired, that maybe it was time for someone else to take my place, or maybe we should close the River North site altogether. It was likely, I said, that I'd be telling the bishop not to reappoint me to Urban Village. It was perhaps the lowest point for me in my ministry. Trey was kind and compassionate and urged me not to make any quick decisions.

Responding to Failure

Obviously, I never made that request to the bishop. So what happened? How did I get out of the trap of comparison and out of that spiral of failure? I did some of the tried and true things that people of faith often do. I took some time away. I went on a retreat. But it was what I did while taking this time away that was most helpful.

Get curious

In her book *Rising Strong,* Brené Brown emphasizes the challenging but necessary step of getting curious about our emotions—feelings of pain, discomfort, shame, and failure. It takes courage to be curious, she notes, because that means we have to explore parts of ourselves that we'd rather gloss over or ignore altogether. It means being vulnerable enough to reflect on statements like, "I'm having an emotional reaction to what's happened, and I want to understand" and questions like, "How do all of these experiences come together to make up who I am?" I took that time away to be curious about myself and to explore why I was so quick to assume the declines were a direct result of my failure as a pastor, assumptions that in turn engendered bitterness toward others—including people on our staff—who were experiencing growth and "success."

Two things helped me that summer. I already mentioned one of them in chapter 2: my journey in reclaiming a sense of belovedness. The other was being curious about and coming to terms with my personality and way of being, specifically my introvertedness. Susan Cain's book *Quiet: The Power of Introverts in a World That Can't Stop Talking* was enormously helpful with this. Cain points out that American culture generally seems to prefer leaders who are extroverts, and I think we in the church world also assume that church planters should be extroverts. I would often ask myself, "Why is it so hard for me to sometimes go to networking events and to 'work a room'? Isn't that what a church planter should do?" I would look at Trey whenever we would go to some sort of event together, and he always seemed able to connect so much more easily than I could. I wouldn't get too down on myself for these things, but they would weigh on me a bit, and those small weights added up over time, creating a growing sense of shame of my tendency to be introverted.

Cain's emphasis on the benefits of introversion, however, and her exploration of the biology of introverts and extroverts was enormously helpful in lifting those weights. In the book, she writes about the studies of Jerome Kagan, a psychologist at Harvard University. In 1989, Kagan and his team started a longitudinal study of infants to see if they could predict who would become introverts and who would become extroverts. When the infants were four months old, the researchers would present each infant with various forms of stimuli, like balloons popping and the scent of alcohol on cotton swabs. The researchers found that about 20 percent of the babies cried lustily and pumped their arms and legs when experiencing the stimuli; these infants were labeled "high-reactive." Forty percent of the infants were quiet and placid ("low-reactive"), and 40 percent fell in between those two extremes. Kagan and his team continued to study the infants as they grew, conducting tests when they were two, four, seven, and eleven years old, and they found that, by and large, the high-reactive babies grew up to be introverts and low-reactive babies were extroverts. In other words, Kagan's studies found that in many cases, we are hard-wired to respond differently to stimuli. There are good reasons introverts like to be in quieter, smaller environments and extroverts like to be in settings where there is more stimulation: extroverts' nervous systems aren't as affected by it. These findings are not always true, of course, but Kagan surmised that introverts and extroverts physiologically respond to stimuli differently.

I distinctly remember reading this section of Cain's book on a beach on the shores of Lake Michigan, and it was like the heavens opened up for me, and Lady Gaga led a chorus in singing, "You were born this way, baby." I started embracing my introversion and stopped envying extroverts. Rather than skipping over Paul's entreaty that we have gifts that differ from one another, I actually started to believe it. I started the very slow process of defining myself by my belovedness and not by personality type or my site's worship attendance numbers.

I wish I could tell you that I'm completely there. I'm not. It's still hard not to measure myself by worship statistics (and compare myself to pastors of other, larger churches), because these measurements become so ingrained into pastors' identities. This identity formation happens pretty quickly in a pastor's career.

When I was still very new in the ministry, I went to a breakfast gathering with other clergy in my district. As I was standing in line, waiting for my turn for the fruit, bagels, and coffee, a seasoned pastor came up behind me and introduced himself. This was a nice gesture, I thought. After I introduced myself and told him where I was serving, his next question was blunt. "So," he said, "what are your stats?"

I was taken aback by the directness of the question. Is this how it's going to be in the ministry? I wondered. That I'm measured only by my "stats"? So I did what any church-planter-in-the-making would do. I fudged a bit and told him they were higher than they were. And, I must confess, I still fudge a bit today. I am, to be sure, a work in progress. But I feel like I have turned a corner in getting a sense of who I am and what I offer as part of the body of Christ.

What's also been helpful about getting curious about myself is that it's allowed me to begin to look back and do autopsies on other personal failure stories and to remove them from subconscious hiding. It's as if I had put these stories into a spooky attic in my mind and had a gatekeeper at the foot of the creaky stairs leading to this attic who kept hauntingly intoning, "Don't go in there!" Curiosity, though, has been the key to ignoring the gatekeeper, and God-given courage has been my flashlight to start exploring and taking second looks.

At the church I pastored before starting Urban Village, one year I thought it would be a good idea to commemorate All Saints' Sunday by not only reading the names of those who had passed away and not only having somber organ music playing underneath the recitation of these names, but also to add one more thing to this ritual: bagpipes! I had recently presided over a funeral, and at the internment at the cemetery, the family had a bagpiper play "Amazing Grace." I thought it was one of the most moving things I had ever heard. Why not hire a bagpiper to do the same thing at an All Saints' service? When I contacted a bagpiper (I still marvel at what you can find on the Internet) and explained what I wanted to do, she said she was available and would be happy to come. But she also told me, "You do know that bagpipes are really loud, right?"

"Sure," I said, forgetting that when I heard the bagpipes at the internment, *we were outside.* Our church's sanctuary wasn't large by any means—it always reminded me of a New England-style Congregational Church—but I was taken with the novelty of playing bagpipes in church.

For some reason, I also thought it would be a good idea for the bagpiper to be a surprise. So when everyone was gathered and the time came near the beginning of the service for the bagpiper to make her entrance, I sat in the chancel area excitedly waiting for those unmistakable sounds to start filling the sanctuary.

You can probably guess what happened. I know I'll never forget the looks on people's faces as the piper started walking down the aisle. Instead of inspiration, I saw pained looks. Some people literally cringed because the music was so loud. Others put their hands to their ears. A few children looked up to their parents and started saying things that I can only imagine went something like this: "Mommy, make it stop!" And to make matters worse, this was already an emotional service, so the melancholy of the pipes seemed to exacerbate feelings of loss.

As I was watching all of this, I kept thinking, "Dear Lord, what have I done?" Soon after that service, I did my best to take this memory of failure and lock it away in that scary attic in my mind. By doing so, however, I failed to ask myself some important questions like, why did I feel the need to bring the bagpiper? That would have been an important thing to ponder, because I would have been forced to ask myself, "Did you introduce this as a way to help others worship God?" I didn't reflect on any of this, probably because I knew the answer would have been closer to, "No. I did it so people would acknowledge me as a creative pastor, willing to try new things." That's an important lesson—making sure worship is not about the exaltation of Christian Coon but about the exaltation of Jesus Christ.

Share your vulnerability

Getting curious about ourselves isn't the easiest thing to do. It's impossible to be completely objective when asking why we're taking failure so personally and why we're letting declining worship attendance define us. That's why it's also necessary to let others into the process by naming this sense of failure. Talking with close friends and a therapist were both immensely helpful in my exploration. As often happens when we shine light on secrets and shame, others then feel permission to be vulnerable and share their struggles, too. Suddenly, we realize we're not alone and burdens are lifted. It's one reason why I was so inspired when I talked to George Linney, founder of Tobacco Trail Church in Durham, North Carolina.

I originally reached out to George because I thought I'd highlight his new church under the "Think Different" section in chapter 4. I read an article about Tobacco Trail a couple years ago, and it attracted my attention as a holy experiment in literally meeting people where they are. In George's case, he meets them on the Tobacco Trail in Durham, North Carolina. More about that in a minute. What immediately drew me to George was his refreshing candor, which was evident two minutes into our phone conversation. I tried to emphasize that my invitation to talk about failure wasn't spurred by my sense that he was a failure, but George understood right away. He laughed and said that Tobacco Trail Church was the "most famous ten-member church in the world."

I was immediately taken aback. Ten members? Surely he's joking. Plus, what kind of church planter is so open and seemingly joyful about having ten members? I soon learned that George didn't (and doesn't) solely define himself by that number, and instead he gleans joy and purpose from the journey. I know that's a bit of a cliché, but his openness and honesty was a revelation.

George founded Tobacco Trail in 2010 in Durham, North Carolina, after feeling called to pastoral ministry but failing to find a home in various denominations and styles of churches. As he thought about full-time ministry, George got a job at a local REI store, and he and his family started attending a local Episcopal church. But as George spent Sunday after Sunday sitting in the pews, he had a sense that God was saying to him, "You don't belong on this side of the altar." George was also an avid biker and runner, and it was during one of his rides that he had what he calls his "Isaiah moment" (see Isaiah 6:1-8). He was out riding on the American Tobacco Trail (a twenty-two-plus-mile rails-to-trails project located near Durham) one day, and he had a sense that God was telling him that there was a church out here, on the trail. Not long after that epiphany, George started gathering people together for worship at different points along the trail, and Tobacco Trail Church was born.

George and his faith community do indeed think different when it comes to many aspects of the traditional church:

- Instead of a building, they typically worship outside on the trail, often meeting at a park. George estimates they've had at least sixty different worship sites. "That's what I call a mega-church," he says. "Since when did the so-called mega-churches get to label themselves?"
- Instead of worshiping weekly, they gather monthly, always with a four-fold model of worship: Gathering, Word,

Practice, and Sending Forth. Because they worship outside, they always prepare themselves for unexpected surprises and people who come upon them and participate. As the church's website notes, "Simply, we get together. We actively listen to scripture and preaching. We participate in the ancient practices of the church such as: The Lord's Supper, Foot Washing, Anointing, and Baptism of new believers. Finally, we are set loose to be God's people in the world and to share the body of Christ in all that we do."

- Many church planters are reticent about sharing their "statistics" if they're not as high as they or denominational officials would want them. Not George. "I'd say a big gathering would consist of fifteen people. We've probably gained and lost twenty to thirty people over the years, and every time someone leaves, it breaks my heart. But even people who leave, I still try to disciple them and be discipled by them," he says.

- Instead of earning a salary only from full-time ministry, George is bi-vocational. Or, perhaps a better way to describe it, "quad-vocational": The bulk of his take-home income comes from marketing work he does for local Fleet Feet stores (a national athletic shoes and apparel chain), and in addition to leading Tobacco Trail Church, he also works with Duke Divinity School first-year students. And, oh yeah, he coaches local runners, too. All of these jobs bring potential for ministry. Tobacco Trail is now affiliated with the Cooperative Baptist Fellowship, which partially funds the church, and its leaders constantly encourage George to be out and about among athletes at races and in the community. Not that he needs the encouragement.

George's enthusiasm for his ministry is infectious, as is his embrace of failure within his ministry. My notes are littered with wonderful aphorisms from George: "We're crushing it, and we're the greatest failure in the ministry of the church"; "Sharing the gospel means having the courage to be misunderstood"; "My failure is God's success"; "Once you get messy, get messier"; "If our church ended tomorrow, God would say that was a great thing."

George and the folks at Tobacco Trail Church think different, and they do it with energy and a passionate desire to share the gospel in all kinds of contexts, recognizing that failure is not only inevitable, but something to be celebrated, even publicized. I can't tell you how refreshing it was to talk to George, as he gave me permission to be honest about my struggles and challenges, too. George's vulnerability was like a conversational door swinging wide open, inviting me to participate, even though we had only just met on the phone.[5]

Find companions

In many ways, this book is an exercise in vulnerability in the hopes that others will be moved to share their failures with friends and colleagues, too. Sadly, we live in a ministerial world that too often prioritizes gamesmanship and unhealthy comparisons. A fair warning, then. If you do have the courage to share your sense of failure with others, it might not always be reciprocated, understood, or appreciated. Awkward silences are not uncommon. Early in my ministry, I went to a daylong gathering of United Methodist clergy (different from the one where I got the "What are your stats?" question), where the focus of the day was on the trials and challenges of local-church ministry. At one point, we were encouraged to get together in groups of three or four.

I don't remember the exact question we were supposed to answer, but I do remember feeling led to share some of the "they didn't teach us some of this stuff in seminary" laments that many new pastors have. I was in a group of seasoned clergy and, after I shared, they immediately started talking about a different topic with zero acknowledgment of my vulnerability and struggle. It was as if I'd said, "Let's discuss Einstein's Theory of Relativity," and they subconsciously agreed to change the subject since they didn't know how to react to my seemingly nonsensical comments.

Being vulnerable and nakedly honest with others can be freeing, then, but it's not always reciprocated. How do we respond when we feel like we're the only resident on Failure Island?

Memorizing and collecting favorite Scripture passages, of course, is a great spiritual practice to cultivate. Many of us can tell stories of faithful parishioners who recite Psalm 23 or Isaiah 43:2 in times of loss or grief, as those passages are wellsprings of strength to draw on when you feel like you have nowhere else to turn. Not surprisingly, given the nature of this book, I've also become a fan of collecting failure stories, too. I don't do it because of a sense of *schadenfreude*, the German word/phrase that speaks to the pleasure that one derives from another person's misfortune (though the fact that I could type that word without having to look up the spelling makes me wonder!). I collect these stories because, if I can't find people who are sensitive to my vulnerability and willingness to be frank about my missteps, the stories remind me that I'm not alone. A great cloud of witnesses of women and men of faith have failed and felt themselves to be frauds.

In chapter 2, I mentioned John Wesley and his well-known "heart strangely warm'd" experience, but I sometimes forget to put that scene in the context of Wesley's failed mission to the colony of Georgia. Those who have read Wesley's history know of his high hopes as he made his way to Georgia in 1735 to share the gospel with Native Americans. To say that things didn't go well may be generous. No one (neither the colonists nor Native Americans) seemed terribly interested in Wesley's brand of Anglican Christianity, and his personal life didn't fare much better, as his infamous romance and breakup with Sophy Hopkey can attest. (Wesley was scorned by dear Sophy, and he responded by calling her out from the pulpit.) In *Heart Strangely Warmed,* Jonathan Dean sums up Wesley's state of mind: "At the beginning of 1738, John and Charles Wesley must have seemed a pathetic pair, washed-up jetsam from a disastrous colonial experiment, whose future and character alike were in question."[6]

On January 24, 1738, Wesley wrote in his journal, "I went to America, to convert the Indians; but oh! Who shall convert me? Who, what is he that will deliver me from this evil heart of mischief? I have a fair summer religion. I can talk well: nay, and believe myself, while no danger is near. But let death look me in the face, and my spirit is troubled."[7]

Five days later, Wesley wrote this: "It is now two years and almost four months since I left my native country in order to teach the Georgian Indians the nature of Christianity. But what have I learned myself in the meantime? Why, what I the least of all suspected, that I who went to America to convert others was never myself converted to God."[8]

Along with countless others, I am inspired by Wesley's risk-taking and entrepreneurial ministry, as well as his honest and frank writings. But I think I find more comfort in knowing that he struggled and fell flat on his face. It's especially helpful to know that he wrote these journal entries a mere four months before his Aldersgate experience. I don't think that's a coincidence. Failure can be just the thing to turn over and fertilize ministerial soil.

Another spiritual giant in my life (and in the lives of many others), whom I mentioned earlier in the book, is Henri Nouwen. As

I work on this book, it's finally dawning on me that it's Nouwen's utter humanity that particularly draws me to him. A great example comes from his book *Sabbatical Journey: The Diary of His Final Year,* which is made up of excerpts of Nouwen's journal during the last year of his life. As I recently re-familiarized myself with the book, I noticed that I had written an exclamation point in the margin next to an early journal entry. This was from September 3, 1995: "So, what about my life of prayer? Do I like to pray? Do I want to pray? Do I spend time praying? Frankly, the answer is no to all three questions. After sixty-three years of life and thirty-eight years of priesthood, my prayer seems dead as a rock. . . . The truth is that I do not feel much of anything when I pray."[9] He went on to acknowledge that he used to have a much stronger sense of a prayer life and "a deep sense of Jesus' presence." On the day he wrote this entry, however, he acknowledged, "I do not feel much, if anything when I pray. . . . I have lived with the expectation that prayer would become easier as I grow older and closer to death. But the opposite seems to be happening. The words *darkness* and *dryness* seem to best describe my prayer today."[10]

Nouwen is certainly not alone among notable spiritual writers who go through spiritual dryness, but it always helps me when I feel any sense of failing in my ministry to go back and remind myself that most, if not all, Christian leaders have failed or felt like failures. One can sense Nouwen's frustration that he *used* to be able to pray, but now he can't. He responded, though, in healthy ways. He wondered if he had himself to blame because of his overactivity but quickly noted that he probably shouldn't blame himself. Instead, he got curious. "The real questions are, 'What are the darkness and the dryness about? What do they call me to?' Responding to these questions might well be the main task of my sabbatical."[11] He decided to do one of the hardest things for any of us when we feel like we've failed: He persevered, perhaps sensing a holy invitation in spite of his uncertainty and trepidation. I'll share more about learning to persevere as one of the benefits (or gifts) of failure in the next chapter, but seeking that loving invitation from God—having faith in that invitation from God—and trusting in God's loving insistence that all will be well and that we do not persevere alone are key responses when faced with failure.

Keep failing

The ability to persevere also means that you're awake to more opportunities to risk and fail and those opportunities come up in lots of different ways. I have found that one of the biggest differences between pastoring a new church plant and established churches is that I do lot more weddings than funerals these days. I'm coming up on seven years at Urban Village, and I've only done one funeral. There have been several weddings, however, and I really do enjoy them. One of my most memorable (and fun) weddings was for a couple (Evan and Tarra) who started attending our church literally days before Evan popped the question. I was pleased and honored to officiate the ceremony in Dallas, Tarra's hometown.

The memory of officiating this wedding will stay with me for numerous reasons, one of them being that it was an education in doing ministry in a cross-racial context. Evan and Tarra are African-American, and I've greatly appreciated the opportunity to have open and honest conversations with them about being black and successful in worlds (like work and school) where they are in the minority and sometimes feel the unspoken pressure to "code switch"—to act in white-created cultures in ways that may not be completely natural for them. They're never false to their own senses of who they are, but in small, subtle ways, they're aware of things they do in order to work and live in contexts slightly different from their own.

One of our core areas of ministry at UVC is to be what we call a "church without walls," specifically, a church that is not just culturally and ethnically diverse, but one that has started down the challenging but necessary journey of being anti-racist. Part of this process, of course, means that we read stories and studies of what it means to be anti-racist. Because of this exploration and education, I have just started to get a sense of white privilege and the culturally innate advantages I have and the culturally innate disadvantages that people of color have.

Here's the thing, though. I can read about it. I can have conversations with people of color (like Tarra and Evan) about it, but I'll never fully know what it feels like. My experience of being part of this wedding, though, gave me a very small inkling of what it means and how awkward it feels to function in a context that's culturally different.

During Tarra and Evan's wedding ceremony, as I stood in front of the wedding guests and read through the liturgy, I would have been culturally blind if I hadn't noticed that the good majority of guests at the ceremony were black. I didn't feel awkward about this because, though there were some slight differences in the ceremony compared to other weddings I officiated where the guests were nearly (or totally) completely white, we used the typical United Methodist liturgy, and the flow and rhythm of the ceremony was familiar.

At the reception, however, I started noticing a change in my own emotions. I wasn't uncomfortable per se, but I was cognizant of the fact that I was in an unfamiliar context. I didn't look like most of the people gathered there, the music was different from what I was used to, and—I can't think of any other way to say it—the cultural exchanges (e.g., greetings, handshakes) were a little unfamiliar to me, too. I feel a little sheepish writing all this, but I think my experience begins to get at what people of color might feel in settings where the cultural norms are slightly different from their norms. By no means am I saying that I now know what people of color feel like in our society, but I did pay attention to my internal insecurities. Even though everyone I talked to made me feel very comfortable and welcome, I was a little nervous about saying or doing the wrong thing.

In other words, I didn't want to be a cultural failure. The best way I knew how to do that was to stay as hidden and inconspicuous as possible. I enjoyed pleasant conversation with the other guests at my table and, while I was enjoying the celebration, I also planned to make an exit as soon as they cut the cake, which also meant that I wouldn't be venturing out on the dance floor.

The fact that I would skip the dancing is a little unusual for me. I like to dance at weddings, and though I wouldn't say I'm a great dancer, I'd like to think I don't embarrass myself. But if my plan was to be inconspicuous, well, let's just say that getting out on the dance floor would work *against* that plan. In my mind, that would simply shine a spotlight on what would surely be a massive fail ("Hey everyone, come look at the forty-seven-year-old white pastor try to dance!"). Some of the music was new to me, and I noticed that everyone on the dance floor moved effortlessly to the beat and in rhythm with everyone around.

As I was eyeing the exits, then, I noticed out of the corner of my eye that Evan's mom was trying to get my attention. She has a gregariousness that is infectious; it's impossible not to feel good about yourself and the world after having a conversation with her. But she was making a request that I wasn't going to accept. She had come off the dance floor and was entreating me to come out and dance with her. Clearly, she didn't know my plan for a quiet exit and my attempt to stay hidden.

Or maybe she did.

No matter what her motives were, she would not be denied and pulled me out to join her on the dance floor. I started (in my mind) awkwardly moving to the music and, to my slight surprise, there was no spotlight shone down on me to point out my failure. Instead, there was encouragement, a few cheers and a couple iPhones recording the moment, not to mock or demean, but to celebrate and affirm. As I was dancing with Evan's mom and everyone around me, one of my favorite children's books that we read to our kids came to mind. The book is called *Giraffes Can't Dance* and is the story of Gerald the giraffe and his self-consciousness about his inability to dance compared to his animal friends. Near the end of the book, though, after a cricket gives Gerald some encouragement to give dancing a chance, Gerald follows the cricket's advice, and he's ecstatic with the results:

Gerald felt so wonderful
his mouth was open wide.
I am dancing! Yes, I'm dancing!
I AM *DANCING!*" Gerald cried.[12]

I felt the same way. If I were judged simply by my dancing skills compared to those around me, of course, I would have rated a "C-" at best. But that wasn't the point. I was out there. I was dancing, unafraid of making a misstep.

This whole scenario came to mind for me as I reflected on the process of moving into a situation where there's a good chance for failure, especially if you're still licking your wounds from previous failures. Evan's mom was like God for me that evening, reaching out to me, insisting that I come out and join the party, and when she held my hands on the dance floor, she was silently affirming that I would not be alone in the midst of the music and uneasiness.

That's the offer that God makes for each of us. It sucks to fail. We have to name that. We cannot glibly spout off phrases such as "Failure makes you stronger" without acknowledging how difficult it is to come back from failure. But we also cannot be paralyzed by the feeling that failure is final.

Here's the thing about those low moments and failures I experienced: *God still did great things.* God still used us to do vital ministry. God still took what we offered and enabled us to have an impact on broken lives. This good news and blessed assurance compels all of us to be curious about our own feelings about failure, name them and know that others experience their own doubts and insecurities, and then watch closely for God's lovingly insistent invitation that we go back out to face (and dance to) the music again.

6

THE GIFTS THAT
FAILURE PROVIDES

The adage "One man's trash is another man's treasure" is a pretty good description of much of the art that hangs on the walls of our home. We do not have banana peels or milk containers proudly displayed over our fireplace, but here's a list of materials that you *can* find: a broken plate, part of an old door, a discarded piece of sheet metal, springs from an abandoned car, and several bottle caps. This list is not exhaustive, but it gives you a hint that we are fans of folk (aka, "outsider") art.

There doesn't seem to be a hard and fast definition of outsider art, but in a 1994 article in the *New York Times*, Roberta Smith noted that "outsider art" is a somewhat vague, catchall term for self-taught artists of any kind.[1] My good friend Jeff was an outsider art dealer at one time and got me interested in it, and I've taken a particular interest in artists who use materials that would otherwise be taken to a garbage dump. Maybe it's because I ply in the resurrection trade, but I feel a connection to inspired individuals who take things that others have left for dead and make something beautiful out of them.

One of our favorite pieces is a work created by Missionary Mary Proctor. Mary started making art after suffering a personal tragedy. In 1995, three members of her family were killed in a house fire and, afterward, Mary sensed that God was telling her to respond to this loss by painting, specifically painting doors. She followed that call and to this day paints doors and other found objects from the junkyard she lives next to. As part of her art, she often writes inspirational messages, all of which come out of her upbringing and her faith. A common subject in her messages is her grandmother—more specifically, the lessons her grandmother shared. Here's the message Mary painted on the piece we own:

My Grandma Old Blue Willow Plates

Oh how I remember so well when I was a child I broke my grandmas old blue willow plates. I thought she would whip me. Instead she held my hands and said "Child I forgive you cause just yesterday God forgave me. He said one must forgive to be forgiven."[2]

To accompany the message, Mary took shards of a broken blue willow plate and arranged and glued the broken pieces to form the torso of the grandmother and child.

This work of art has always spoken to me. I love the way it takes brokenness and transforms it into beauty, honesty, and grace. When I bought it, I figured it would have one singular use: to provide me with inspiration whenever I reflected on it.

Over the years, however, I've discovered that it's had a much broader and more diverse impact. Visitors would be moved by it when they came into my office and saw it on the wall (back when I had an office in a church building!). Young ones would gaze closely at it when I would bring it out for a children's sermon. And now that it hangs in our family room, it has become a sacred reminder of God's presence for my children, too. I was surprised the other day when my son rattled off what the painting says as if he were reciting the Lord's Prayer. The words have been embedded in his heart, and who knows what impact they'll have as he grows older.

Mary's inspired creativity is a good way to introduce this final chapter. I've written some about the benefits of failure, but when pressed to actually name those benefits, we usually offer a general description that goes something like, "Failure shows us how not to do something, so we can improve in the future." There's truth in that, but I believe failure can provide more gifts than we realize. Just as this piece of art has had a greater impact than simply inspiring me, so does failure do more than just provide an improved set of instructions to complete a task.

Paul names various gifts of the spirit in Romans 12:6-8, and in the section right after these verses, he shares a list of maxims that has been called the marks of a true Christian. Whenever I need a reminder of the kind of person I should be as a follower of Jesus, Romans 12:9-21 is a good refresher course. It starts out with "Let love be genuine" and ends with "Do not be overcome with evil, but overcome evil with good," and in between (depending on how one splits them up) are more than twenty short rules for life for Christians. These rules, I believe, can also be interpreted as gifts that demonstrate that failure does not have the final word. These gifts include authenticity, faith, hope, perseverance, hospitality, and humility.

Authenticity: "Let Love Be Genuine" (Romans 12:9a)

When friends found out that I was working on a book about failure, I started to receive occasional articles from them to help my project along. One of my favorite articles was about Johannes Haushofer, a professor at Princeton University. Normally, academics put together a *curriculum vitae* that summarizes and highlights only their scholarly accomplishments (*anyone* who puts a resume together understandably focuses only on their accomplishments!). Haushofer has done that, but he's also done something else. He's published a resume of failures and posted it online. This resume includes "degree programs he didn't get into, research funding he didn't receive, and paper rejections from academic journals."[3] Haushofer said he first started publishing his failures in 2011 as a way to support a friend who'd had a professional setback. "I'm hoping that [the failure resume] will be a source of perspective at times when things aren't going well, especially for students and my fellow young researchers," he said. I don't know how Haushofer's students feel about him, but, if our experience at Urban Village is any indication, they appreciate his honesty and genuineness. We recently were reminded of the importance of these qualities when we went through a major staff transition.

We had to go through the very challenging process of replacing Trey at the end of 2015, as he had announced in August that he would be moving to England. In addition to co-leading Urban Village with me, Trey was the pastor at our Wicker Park site. Obviously it was impossible to find someone who replicated Trey's many gifts, but I had several one-on-one meetings with lay leaders at Wicker Park to ask them what qualities they desired in their next pastor. There was a clear characteristic that nearly every person named: authenticity. I was pleased to hear this, as authenticity was something we wanted incorporated into all facets of our ministry, including worship.

Trey and I decided from the beginning of Urban Village that we wanted to include lay testimony as a part of every worship service, and we didn't want people to come up front and simply share how great things may have been going in their lives. We wanted to create an environment where people felt they could share their whole selves, warts, failures, and all. All of UVC's pastors have tried to model this vulnerability in our preaching, and all the Wicker Park folks said how much they appreciated Trey's willingness when he preaches to share his screw-ups and missteps. Trey's willingness to do so is authenticity at its best. That authenticity is, I think, part of the genuine love that Paul speaks of in this Roman text. I smiled when I read that the original Greek for this passage literally is translated not as "Let love be genuine," but simply "Love—genuine!"[4] It's as if Paul knows that the words "love" and "genuine" are deep and strong enough that no participles are necessary.

When we first came to Portland, Maine, to start a new church, we wanted to have our gatherings in public space to lower the barriers for people of all kinds. We arranged to use the meeting room at a local restaurant. We tried to figure out what the best format would be.

We had heard of the video curriculum "Living the Questions" but had never used it. We previewed it a bit and decided it was worth a shot. We made postcards to advertise the group. We created a Facebook event. We put all our energy and effort into launching this study. We even bought matching binders for everyone to put their worksheets in. We had a few new people show up and a few people who were already connected, but the whole thing felt so awkward, academic, and inauthentic. We decided to abandon the whole thing after the first night.

—Sara Ewing-Merrill
Pastor, HopeGateWay Community of Faith, Portland, ME

Thankfully, it's not just our pastors who try to exhibit this vulnerability. In many ways, it's our laity who have taken the lead on sharing in this way and have done so from our first worship services. It's not unusual for one of our testifiers to talk about an addiction or a struggle with loneliness or just general brokenness. Just this past week, Jada talked about her struggle in feeling like an imposter as a Christian and in her academic studies. The week before that, a man named Christian shared about the challenge of living in an Iowa college town as a gay Puerto Rican man. The week before that, Jim testified to the pain of going through a divorce. And the week before that, Ty was open about how his grand post-college vocational plan fell through.

It's not unusual for a person in worship to seek out the testifier after the service to talk further with him or her. I don't think any of the testifiers explicitly said, "I failed," but, in a sense, they share a bit of their own "resumes of failure," and when they do, a barrier to personal communication has been lifted. The testifier is saying, "I don't have it all together, but I'm still here in this community, wanting to give and receive the kind of genuine love that doesn't play games and doesn't hide behind false images."

Authentic and genuine love—love that allows us the freedom to share our failures—creates a pathway that leads to deeper relationships with others in a community. When you hear someone say they don't have their stuff together—especially because we live in a culture that prizes superficial happiness—it exhibits the kind of broken and genuine love that Jesus exemplified. And what a gift that is.

Faith: "Hold Fast to What Is Good" (Romans 12:9c)

I recently read an article by Carey Nieuwhof entitled, "Cool Church Isn't What It Used to Be" on the Lewis Center for Church

Leadership website, and he advises churches that they cannot merely add contemporary music and great stage lighting in order to grow their congregation.[5] In addition, he says it's impossible to try to be cutting-edge because "cutting-edge" changes so quickly. I agree with him, but it's still a temptation to fall into the trap of being (choose your adjective) hip, edgy, and/or exceptional.

One of the tasks for starting a new church in the city is trying to find a place to have worship. It's one of the biggest challenges of planting, and it's not as easy as it may seem. Not only do you need to find a space large enough to hold a certain number of people, but you also don't want it to be *too* large. You need space for children's activities and, ideally, space for storage. You need to figure out where you'd put food and coffee out and, in Chicago, you need to be fairly close to a train station or major bus route. Parking would be great, but that's a luxury, not necessarily a necessity.

When we were ready to launch Urban Village's third site in Chicago's Andersonville neighborhood, we marked out the boundaries within which we would look for a worship space and hit the streets. There was one possibility that presented itself quickly: a retirement facility/nursing home that has United Methodist roots and is centrally located in the Andersonville neighborhood. The facility has hosted Northern Illinois Conference events in the past so we certainly knew about it, and they graciously offered to be the worship location of our Andersonville site at a very low rate. We were grateful for their generosity, but . . . well . . . it was a nursing home. It didn't necessarily communicate edginess so we said thank you, but gave a kind of "don't call us, we'll call you" answer as we went looking for something a little more hip.

We looked and looked and looked. Theaters, schools, art studios, bars; nothing was a fit either logistically or financially. We thought we had a possibility in a room in a Chicago Park District facility, but when a group of us went to check it out, we realized that the room was directly over a gymnasium that would be in use on Sunday mornings. We sent one of our folks down there to bounce some balls and make some noise to test it out and realized that we really wouldn't be able to hear anyone speaking (though I've preached a few sermons where congregants may have counted that as advantage).

After striking out numerous times, we came to the conclusion that the nursing home might have to be the place so we decided to give it a shot. We launched in the fall of 2011, and since then, it's been one of our strongest sites. To be sure, there are times when it has some drawbacks, but there have been many more positives that have come out of this relationship, including the formation of some wonderful relationships with residents in the home. Some of our ministries with residents have included UVC members bringing in their dogs for "Yappy Hour," a time of canine (and human) fellowship; planting an organic garden; and participating in the home's glee club. Our failure to find what we thought would be the "cool" space was a reminder that we have to put our faith in something (or, rather, Someone) other than worship location. Brittany Isaac, the Andersonville site pastor, told me that numerous people have come up to her and said it was *because* the space was unhip that they knew our church was different. The focus isn't on the appearance of some perfect building but on the people and ministry. This place focuses on the right things.

One of the biggest temptations when starting something new is to depend solely on something or someone other than God. The most common mistake is depending only on your own gifts and graces, believing that the only reason this ministry is going to take off is because of your own charisma or indefatigable work ethic. If the mistake is not depending on yourself, it's depending on the latest ministry trend or, in our case, depending on an edgy worship space. When all of these things inevitably fail you in one way or another, that's often the reminder about where your faith and dependence should lie.

In this passage from Romans, Paul tells us to hold fast to what is good. Other translations say to "hold on for dear life" or "cleave" to what is good. This, I think, is ultimate dependence, ultimate faith: To hold on for dear life to the One who is the ultimate good. We have numerous reminders of God's goodness in the Scriptures, especially the Psalms ("Praise the Lord, for the Lord is good; sing to his name for he is gracious" [Psalm 135:3]), and those reminders are, indeed, good news after we have put our faith in something else.

That's one of the clear messages in the Prodigal Son story. The son believes he has a sense of what is truly good and gambles everything on those things: his inheritance, travel, a carefree lifestyle, and his ability to earn a living. He finally, as the text says, comes to himself, and realizes he has been depending on the wrong things. In a recent article in the *Christian Century* about making sure God is at the center of one's life, Peter Marty noted that "if we place ourselves at the center of importance—our ego, pride, or achievements—we go nowhere significant, spiritually speaking at least."[6] This is how the son failed: He put himself at the center of importance. He then can think of only one place that he can truly depend on and have faith in: his home. Even then, of course, he's not completely sure, but something compels him to set off and he's welcomed.

Sometimes we come to God as a last resort, often when we've tried everything else, but even then our good God receives us. When this happens, we are reminded of God's faith in us, which is itself a tremendous gift. That gift, in turn, is a powerful reminder that we can and should place our trust and faith in God, the only sure and rock-solid foundation in our lives, the basis for hope in times of failure. The second stanza of the classic hymn, "My Hope Is Built," summarizes this well:

> When darkness veils his lovely face, I rest on his unchang-
> ing grace.
> In every high and stormy gale, my anchor holds within
> the veil.
> On Christ the solid rock I stand,
> all other ground is sinking sand;
> all other ground is sinking sand.

Failure is a harsh, but sometimes necessary, reminder that God's faith in us is abiding. Failure also shows us that we have the capacity (the gift!) for placing our full trust not in sinking sand, but on a solid rock.

Hope: "Rejoice in Hope" (Romans 12:12a)

One of Urban Village's tried-and-true marketing/evangelism efforts is something very basic: putting up flyers around the neighborhood. In these days of new and exciting ways to reach people via the Internet, putting up flyers seems kind of pedes-trian and boring, especially when the flyer is put on a community bulletin board where there are dozens of other flyers vying for a person's attention. We've tried to get creative over the years and put the flyers up in places that will get noticed (sometimes they're too noticeable: someone from the Chicago Streets & Sanitation Department called me a couple years ago to threaten a fine if we put any more flyers under windshield wipers or on telephone poles), but we also know that flyering is only mildly successful at best. Still, it's inexpensive, and it's a good exercise in hope, or at least some slightly diluted version of hope: we put up a flyer and then say a quick prayer that goes something like, "I hope someone sees this and comes to church!"

Christian hope, of course, is much richer than mere wishful thinking, and it's much bolder than spending time fantasizing about one's future. I confess I too often engage in hope only when I feel good about my faith and/or if I'm content with the state of the church I'm pastoring. Hope is more radical than that. Douglas John Hall notes that hope is one of faith's many dimensions. "(Hope) is faith applied to the future . . . one trusts the future to *God*—not to oneself, not to humankind as a whole, not to government, not to the church, not to history, not to some theory of progress, but to God."[7] Hope means that I trust the future to God, *no matter what kind of state my faith is in*, even in the midst of despair, struggle, and, yes, failure.

A good example of biblical hope is found in Jeremiah. In chapter 29, Jeremiah is writing a letter to the exiles, who were forced to relocate to Babylon in 597 BCE. The exiles were feeling the weight of God's judgment. They had been driven out of their homes in Jerusalem by the Babylonian oppressors, and I'm sure were doing some deep reflection on how they got to where they were. Where did they go wrong? How did everything fall apart so completely? I can't imagine a more hope-less situation than one where two things you felt like you could depend on—your faith and your home—had been taken away. And yet Jeremiah informs them that this is the *perfect* time to hope. In this foreign land of seeming God-forsakenness, the exiles are told not to despair, but to build houses, plant gardens (and eat the fruit of those gardens), raise families, and, against anyone's better judgment, seek the welfare of this oppressive city where they now lived. When all seems lost, Jeremiah says, that's when we have the most reason to hope. "For surely I know the plans I have for you, says the Lord, plans for your welfare and not for harm, to give you a future with hope" (Jeremiah 29:11).

This runs completely counter to how I used to think about hope because hope is usually the last thing that comes to mind in the midst of despair and failure. Anger? Yes. Bitterness? Absolutely. Doubt? Come on in. But hope? Yes, hope, because hope is a lot more robust and tenacious than we give it credit for.

I think for some of us (myself included at times), hope conjures up images of starry-eyed dreamers who clutch lucky coins and throw them into a heavenly fountain. But hope is more than that. It can boldly, radically, surprisingly show up when failure has seemingly had the last word. Biblical hope scoffs at permanent failure because it reminds us that we are ultimately a people of the empty tomb, not an oppressor's sentence of death.

You may know Maya Angelou's poem and novel, *I Know Why the Caged Bird Sings,* but that phrase was not originally hers. It belonged to one of the first great black poets of the twentieth century, Paul Laurence Dunbar.

One of Dunbar's first poems was "Sympathy," which, the Poetry Foundation's web site notes, expresses the dismal plight of blacks in America. Here's the last stanza of that poem:

> I know why the caged bird sings, ah me,
> When his wing is bruised and his bosom sore,—
> When he beats his bars and he would be free;
> It is not a carol of joy or glee,
> But a prayer that he sends from his heart's deep core,
> But a plea, that upward to Heaven he flings—
> I know why the caged bird sings![8]

This poem could reflect any of the gifts that failure can bring about, though, of course, Dunbar was speaking of the failure of

American systems that oppressed and excluded him and the black community. Dunbar sees this bird with bruised wing and sore bosom, that beats his bars to be free. That, to me, is a pretty great description of hope. Dunbar shares another powerful thought about hope in his book, *The Strength of Gideon: And Other Stories*: "Hope is tenacious. It goes on living and working when science has dealt it what should be its deathblow."[9] I certainly don't want to equate my personal failures with the racism that Dunbar experienced, but I'm grateful for these words. When failure seemingly erects bars that limit one's capacity, that's when hope—battered, bruised hope—really shows up.

I mentioned putting up flyers earlier. It seems to work better in some neighborhoods than others, and it's probably had the most success in and around the neighborhood where our Wicker Park site is located. Soon after we launched that site, we made the flyering rounds to coffee houses, sandwich shops, and even an occult bookstore (Trey tells a great story about the dumbfoundedness of the clerk in that bookstore when he asked if we could leave UVC flyers there . . . and her eventual agreement).

When you put flyers up, of course, (and this is a downside of flyering) more than a few end up in the trash or on the ground. But even a flyer on the ground still communicates hope and promise. A man named Paul Ortiz was walking in the Wicker Park neighborhood one day and noticed one of those sad little flyers on the ground. He had been thinking a lot about his faith, wondering where God was leading him, wrestling with his vocation. He picked the flyer up off the asphalt. Something about it spoke to him. He, his wife, and little daughter checked out this church that said they love Democrats and Republicans, gay people and straight people, tattoos and suits.

They started coming to the Sunday night services, housed in an old Lutheran church. They stuck with it when numbers started dwindling and worshipers moved the service down to the basement. They stayed faithful when it moved to a different location and started to grow. He paid attention when sensing a call to seminary and the ministry. And, as I write this, he will be moving to Tacoma, Washington, to help plant a United Methodist Church among people who also need to experience the hope only a discarded flyer covered with dirty footprints can proclaim.

Perseverance: "Persevere in Prayer" (Romans 12:12c)

I noted in the last chapter the increase of weddings that I officiate these days and that includes ceremonies that I perform for personal friends and family. I was blessed to give the homily at my godson's wedding last New Year's Eve, and I focused on the common wedding text of 1 Corinthians 13. Even though I've done plenty of weddings with this passage as the main text, I still find little treasures tucked into the verses (thank you, Holy Spirit!). I was reflecting on verses 4-7 ("Love is patient; love is kind . . .) when the last three words of this section struck me. Verse 7 reads, "(Love) bears all things, believes all things, hopes all things, endures all things."

Endures all things. Endures? I'm not sure Hallmark is going to make much money on wedding or anniversary cards that communicate the message, "What a joy to endure this marriage with you." Often when we hear that word, we think of something we have to tolerate or slog through, like, "We endured that math class" or "Hang in there and endure this sermon." But endurance does not have to be a negative thing. My copy of *Westminster Dictionary of Theological Terms* says that endurance is "the Christian's perseverance in the Christian life through all things as sustained by God's grace."[10] Perseverance and endurance remind us that we're sustained by God's grace.

I think perseverance is one of the most underrated qualities in the Christian life. The word comes from the Latin *perseverare,* which means to "continue steadfastly, persist." There's something noble in continuing steadfastly after you fail. The famous quotation by Teddy Roosevelt in his "The Man in the Arena" speech addresses this. Roosevelt said that it is not the critic who should get the glory, but "the man who is actually in the arena," the one "who errs, who comes short again and again, because there is no effort without error and shortcoming; but who does actually strive to do the deeds." If the man succeeds, he knows triumph, but even if he fails, he should be lauded: "If he fails, at least fails while daring greatly, so that his place shall never be with those cold and timid souls who neither know victory nor defeat."[11]

It's a stirring quote and emphasizes that it is the attempt, the trying and getting up and trying again, that is noteworthy. While I certainly agree with all of this, there's something more to Christian perseverance: When you continue on after failing, there's the opportunity to discover greater spiritual riches farther into the process, riches you would have missed if you had initially succeeded. By "spiritual riches," I don't necessarily mean success as society defines it, but a deeper and more vibrant connection to God and a greater realization of God's faithfulness.

Franciscan priest and author Richard Rohr encapsulates this in his reflections on prayer and meditation in his book *Dancing Standing Still.* In talking about contemplation, Rohr says that this practice is more than just daydreaming, but is "the flowering of patience and steady perseverance. . . . It seems to me that true progress, or the hope that we have, is not naively optimistic, a straight line, or without regression. Spiritual progress, ironically, develops through tragedy and through falling."[12] As C. G. Jung said, "Where we stumble and fall is where we find pure gold," the gold of the gospels, the hidden gold of our own souls, and then the beautiful soul of the whole creation.

Spiritual progress comes through tragedy and falling and rising again, a truth that is both harrowing and hopeful. Harrowing because we the fear the pain of tragedy and failure. Hopeful because tragedy and failure can also lead us, as Rohr says, to the gold of the gospels. We have a clearer realization that ours is a God whose steadfast presence will never leave us when we fall. I don't think we truly capture the depth of the truth of this steadfastness when we only know success. "A person's steps are made secure by the LORD when they delight in his way," says the psalmist. "Though they trip up, they won't be thrown down, because the LORD holds their hand." (Psalm 37:23-24, CEB) We don't know the strength of God's hands unless we trip up, and we won't *truly* know the strength of those hands unless we persevere, when we get up and trip up again and again.

I went rock climbing with my brother-in-law Jud many years ago. I wasn't sure this was a hobby I'd take to, since I don't have the spiritual gift of loving heights, but I was intrigued by Jud's interest in this activity and am usually game to try something new, so we headed to a local state park and found a natural rock formation to scale.

Jud and I climbed using the style known as top rope climbing. Wikipedia defines top rope climbing as "a style in climbing in which a rope, used for the climber's safety, runs from a belayer at the foot of a route through one or more carabiners connected to an anchor system at the top of the route and back down to the climber, usually attaching to the climber by means of a harness." Jud noted, "That allows the belayer to watch the climber's progress and offer guidance and encouragement!"

A belayer is the non-climber who is essentially acting as an anchor and as a guide for the climber. The belayer makes sure there is enough slack in the rope for the climber to climb, but not too much, so if the climber falls, it isn't very far. The belayer also is usually anchored to some other immovable object (like a tree) so that he or she isn't solely dependent on his or her own weight to support the climber in case the climber falls. In my case, it wasn't *if* the climber would fall, but *when*.

Even though I trusted Jud and his belaying expertise, I was a bit tentative as I started my climb. I had never done anything like this before, so even though my mind was telling me this was perfectly safe, the sweat on my palms told a different story. I started making my way up the wall, placing my hands and feet in (what seemed to me) impossibly tiny crevices. I grew a little more confident as I climbed higher and higher, but still I kept wondering if the rope would *really* hold me if I fell? I eventually found out as my foot slipped from a small ledge and I experienced that sickening feeling of falling. That feeling was very brief, however, because the rope held me up, and I was soon able to come back to the wall and keep climbing.

With each subsequent slip and fall (and there were several), I trusted the process more and more. To be sure, it was a little embarrassing to be swinging back and forth like a pendulum after each fall, but I got a little more confident and a little more adventurous each time I tried scaling the wall again. I had faith that despite the embarrassment of slipping (and a few scrapes and cuts that came with each slip), the rope, Jud, and Jud's anchor would hold me. That tested faith strengthened my climbing and gave me the confidence to try different routes up the wall.

Jud (one of the most humble Jesus followers I know) wrote an email to me, sharing some wonderful wisdom about what the rope represents: "The rope does not insulate the climber from injuries to body or ego, but it gives a level of confidence that allows one to push oneself into new and risky territory. The rope is also recognition that no individual climber can master, control, or even know all possible risks. A rock from above may fall, a handhold may give way, weather may change suddenly, a really big bug may appear from the crack next to your face . . . and no amount of skill, practice, confidence, and determination can account for all eventualities. The rope reminds us not to place too much faith in ourselves and our control over any given situation."[13]

I believe that our churches need to discover their own ropes and make full use of them as failing and then persevering in ministry is a powerful revealer of God's faithfulness. That revelation only gets clearer with each subsequent risk and attempt.

To be sure, discernment must be partnered with perseverance. An article I read argued that, "The definition of insanity is trying the same thing over and over again and expecting different results" (attributed to Albert Einstein, though no one knows for sure if he said it) may be the most overused cliché of all time. But just because something is a cliché doesn't mean it's not true.

Perseverance does not mean that a person should keep blindly trying something over and over again even if there's little to no fruit to show for it. All the tools of discernment—prayer, conversations with colleagues, consultations with a ministry coach (which I highly recommend and is something that UVC has utilized from our beginnings)—must be used. We had to go through this kind of discernment when our Wicker Park site was in decline.

Wicker Park was our second site, and we launched it on Sunday nights in the sanctuary of a Lutheran Church six months after the launch of our first site in the South Loop neighborhood. The launch was promising, but both the numbers and the energy started declining after a few months. We persevered and tried different things to reverse the trend, but not much seemed to work. It got to a point where only fifteen to twenty people were worshiping in the basement of the church and knew we were at a crossroads.

Should we continue on or conduct a funeral for the Wicker Park location? Trey took the lead for this discernment process. His recommendation was to give it one more shot, but he also suggested moving to a different building (a theater) within the neighborhood and worshiping on Sunday mornings, not Sunday evenings. He led a small, but faithful team of folks toward this relaunch, and his discernment and perseverance paid off. Wicker Park is now our largest site.

Stories of perseverance at Urban Village, however, don't always have a happy ending. We have numerous occasions when, for example, continued attempts at developing a small group or making contact with a lapsed parishioner via text messages go nowhere. But we usually find the gold of the gospel somewhere in the midst of our efforts. Our annual Ash Wednesday outreach is a prime example.

More and more churches are offering ashes to individuals on the streets every Ash Wednesday (and we took the idea from the Episcopalians). We go out to several highly trafficked areas throughout the city and teams of two or three show up with signs ("Got ashes?"), ashes, and plenty of perseverance. Our hope is that if a person isn't attending an Ash Wednesday service somewhere, they might be curious to find out what we're doing and learn a bit about what Lent is and what it means to be both created by God and created from dust. In other words, what it means to be human. The perseverance is needed because most people take a pass on getting ashed.

One of the places I usually go is Daley Plaza, in the heart of Chicago. The first year we did ashes, I went rather unwillingly. We were still pretty new as a church so we didn't have many people volunteer, but Trey encouraged us all to engage in this activity and be witnesses on the streets. As Trey described what this would entail—standing on street corners, asking people if they wanted ashes for Ash Wednesday—my introvertedness staged a mild protest, and I thought, "I think I'm going to pass on this." As we got closer and closer to Ash Wednesday, I had a sense that the Holy Spirit was trying get through to me with a loving, compassionate message: get over yourself and get out there. So I did and it turned out to be revelatory. For one thing, it built up my evangelistic chops and my boldness for the gospel, but it's also been a good exercise in perseverance. This past Ash Wednesday was no exception.

Easter was early in 2016, which meant that my ash-mate Charlie and I were standing out on the corner of Dearborn Avenue and Washington Street on a cold February morning, braving the winds that would gust across Daley Plaza. I've done this now for six years so I've gotten used to calling out to people: "Ashes for Ash Wednesday?!? We have ashes for all!" At first, it's always a little scary, but it's invigorating, too, to do something outside your comfort zone. A few minutes into this activity, though, I usually ask myself: why am I doing this again? I ask the question because (a) it's cold, and (b) most people don't stop (failure), so I wonder how silly we must look. I think more deeply about the question: why am I doing this again?

This is often a good precursor of a question before one decides to persevere. If you have no compelling reason to continue on in the face of failure, why do it? Failure, then, forces me to answer the question. I'm doing this again because Ash Wednesday, among other things, is a reminder of our humanity, our flesh, which is both tinged with the breath of our Creator God and the dust of the earth. In our virtual worlds, the importance of thinking deeply about our flesh is a message worth sharing so that people know they're more than their Facebook profile.

That's a message worth persevering for, and it kept Charlie and me out on the corner offering this message to anyone who came by. Some did stop, which made persevering worth the cold and rejection. One man dressed in an expensive suit asked a couple questions about Ash Wednesday and its meaning before agreeing to be ashed. As I recited the words and as my pinkie made the shape of the cross on his forehead, he closed his eyes and then looked at me with wonder. He thanked me and then went on with his day. Five minutes later, he returned.

"I don't know if you remember, but you just did the ashes on my forehead a few minutes ago," he said to me.

"I do remember."

"Well, I just felt compelled to come back and tell you that what you're doing out here . . . it's a great thing. We all need it. Thank you."

Not long after that exchange, another man that I judged to be homeless came up and pulled up his stocking cap to reveal that he had already been ashed. I commented on the cross and said that I hoped he had a blessed Lent. But he insisted that he be ashed one more time. I had never done a "double ashing" before, but clearly this was a man who wanted to be reminded of dust and dirt and life. Perhaps he also wanted to be given the encouragement to persevere. So I asked his name and ashed him again, saying a blessing for him and murmuring a prayer of gratitude for myself and for the gift of perseverance.

Hospitality: "Extend Hospitality to Strangers" (Romans 12:13c)

"Putting up shelves shouldn't be too hard, should it? What could go wrong?"

Those two questions entered my mind as my wife and I stood in the Container Store, deliberating whether to purchase a shelving system. When we moved into the city into a townhome, we had to do some downsizing and reallocating of space to store some of our things. Our one-car garage, therefore, became our basement, which meant our car was banished to the elements. We couldn't just leave all these boxes on the floor of the garage, however, and decided to buy some shelves. I didn't realize how sophisticated (and expensive) shelving had become with all kinds of options and designs. We eventually selected the system we wanted and then we were informed that we could pay extra to have a Container Store expert come and install the shelving for us.

This was a tempting offer because it's become a running joke in our household about how unhandy I am. I can do some very basic jobs around the house and have had some minor successes at plumbing fixtures, but, if my wife doesn't think she can handle a fix-it job either, we call the experts.

As we stood in the store, however, and the salesperson gave us the cost of bringing the person in to install the shelving, I'm sure I let out an audible gasp at the price, and that's when those two questions popped into my head. How hard could it be? What could go wrong?

We cleared everything out of our garage and went to work following instructions and measuring the space along our wall. Things seemed to go fairly well at first. It was taking longer than I thought it would, but the initial results were promising. We'd install a few shelves and take a step back and I'd say, "That's pretty good" because "pretty good" is A+ work for me when it comes to home maintenance. The next step, of course, was actually testing the shelves. I had a vague notion that the shelves had a certain weight limit and so I kind of kept that in mind, but I started to get swept up in the moment and started loading more and more boxes onto the shelves. I'd lift a few up, take a step back, look at any gaps in between the boxes and think, "Oooh, I bet we can fit those ice skates in there, too" or "Hmm, this wet vac isn't *that* heavy" and keep cramming things in there, tempting the fate of the shelving system gods.

You can probably see where this is going. I had just finished one wall and then started putting up the shelving on the other wall when I heard the predictable and very loud crash. The weight of all those boxes (and one wet vac and pair of ice skates) was too much for even this sophisticated shelving system and, like the wall of Jericho, it all came a-tumblin' down.

Sometimes I'm able to look at something gone awry and laugh at it because it's all you can do in the moment. You may recall my entreaty in chapter 4 to not to be too earnest in the face of failure. This was not one of those times. I may or may not have picked up some of the empty boxes that the shelving came in and slammed them to the floor repeatedly. I also may or may not have shouted some robust epithets that probably made our new neighbors wonder just who *was* this new family that moved in and do we need to invest in soundproof walls? All that work. All that *pride* in that work was now scattered on the floor, and I would have to start over again.

I really should have known better. It's only common sense that metal shelves secured into drywall can only hold so much. When it comes to making the best use of your space, one also needs to remember that shelving space needs . . . space.

When I outlined this chapter, I intended to have separate sections for humility and hospitality, but the more I thought about these two marks of the true Christian, the more I realized that they go together quite nicely.

Paul advises his readers in this section of Romans to not be haughty nor claim to be wiser than you are. *The Message* translation, as it often does, makes it more plain: "Don't be stuck up. Don't be the great somebody."

Failure reminds me that there's really one Great Somebody, and I should probably respect that rather than believing that the great somebody is me. Failures of all shapes and sizes, whether they happen doing ministry or putting up shelving in your garage, bring us the gift of humility, and we need to explore that deeply because leaders can believe that they're being humble when actually they're really not.

I wrote in the last chapter about the process of our site move from the South Loop to a new neighborhood. After we had spent several months in our new space, and it became clear that this move may have been a mistake, and we might have to move yet again, I wrote a fairly long treatise that I intended to share with the congregation, summarizing the state of our site and how we were going to respond. In the midst of writing this summary, I fell into the trap of trying to be accountable while in reality I was taking too much responsibility.

In these days when transparency, accountability, and authenticity are prized virtues in leaders, we sometimes hear of a leader taking responsibility for a failure and using a variation of President Harry Truman's famous motto that "the buck stops here." People seem to admire leaders—be they football coaches or CEOs—who are accountable rather than passing the metaphorical buck. I did the same thing in writing this summary. I took responsibility and much of the blame, thinking, "This is what leaders do. The buck stops with me."

I shared this treatise with a few of my leaders before I sent it to the rest of the congregation, however, and consistently received the same response: quit apologizing. They were reminding me that this situation wasn't all about my perceived failure in leadership because I wasn't the only one who made this decision. Other lay leaders had also agreed to this move, and these responses made me realize that I had succumbed to a false sense of humility. In many ways, taking all the blame and seeing this as my failure was the opposite of humility. It was, in fact, rather egotistical, as if saying that any success *or* failure is all about me. The lay leaders reminded me that other people (and other factors) were in the room, and I needed to make space for them rather than shoving myself into every situation.

To be sure, there are leaders who *do* need some humility and need to be accountable. But exhibiting humility by taking sole responsibility isn't the right direction either. Some things are out of our control no matter how hard we work or how faithful we are and it takes some humility to realize that. The key, again, is to make space for God and not try to cram yourself into every nook and cranny in your ministry. And that's how I see a connection to hospitality.

I'm grateful for what seems to be a surge of books and articles in recent years reclaiming the art and ministry of hospitality. In most churches, of course, "hospitality" means providing cookies, juice, and coffee for post-worship snacks. Like hope, though, hospitality is a much more robust word than our usual conception. Christine Pohl, in her book, *Making Room: Recovering Hospitality as a Christian Tradition,* does an excellent job of not only giving a history of hospitality but also sharing compelling reasons for why true hospitality is a *necessity* for any ministry. "Hospitality is not optional for Christians, nor is it limited to those who are specially gifted for it," she writes.[14] Her definition of hospitality helped spur my thinking about failure as a reminder to make space for God and others: "By definition, hospitality involves some space into which people are welcomed, where unless the invitation is given, the stranger would not feel free to enter."[15]

One of the most powerful examples of hospitality as it pertains to Jesus in the Scriptures comes in the story about the disciples' walk to Emmaus (Luke 24:13-35). After the resurrected Christ comes alongside two disciples who were walking down the road, hears their stories and then shares some insights of his own, the disciples make space for a person they believe to be a stranger: "But they urged him strongly, saying, 'Stay with us, because it is almost evening and the day is now nearly over.' So he went in to stay with them" (Luke 24:29). After he accepts their invitation and gathers at table with them, they break bread with and their eyes are opened to see who is in their midst. I don't think I'm alone in failing to make space for Christ every single day, which means that my eyes aren't opened to his presence. One of our Urban Village kids reminded me of this just last Sunday when she made up her own liturgy when offering the bread to those coming forward to communion. "It's Jesus bread. Have fun!" This is a child of God who was making space for the resurrected Christ!

One of the main non-profits that we partnered with at the beginning of Urban Village's history was Inspiration Corporation (IC), an organization that both provides meals for the hungry and homeless and also trains aspiring cooks and chefs to work in the food and restaurant industry. One early Saturday morning a few years ago, a group of us were going to meet in the Woodlawn neighborhood on Chicago's South Side to volunteer at one of IC's locations that served free breakfasts.

I, like many other followers of Christ, often sense his presence when serving and working with the poor so I was looking forward to volunteering, but, truth be told, I was also rubbing the sleep out of my eyes as I shuffled onto the train to make my way south. About one or two stops into the trip, I noticed a man and a woman, each dressed in rumpled clothing, sitting next to me with two big grocery bags. I hadn't paid close attention to them at first, but the noise they were making when rustling through the bags made them hard to ignore. The man pulled out a loaf of Wonder white bread and set it on his lap. The woman pulled out a package of Oscar Mayer bologna and little packets of mayonnaise and mustard and they proceeded to use their laps as a table on which to prepare this feast. At first, I was a little incredulous. They're making sandwiches on the train? Can they do that? But I quickly stopped worrying if any regulations were being broken because I assumed they were homeless and simply making a meal, so who was I to stop them? I closed my eyes to see if I could sleep a bit more before coming to my stop where I would make my way to volunteer and do a Good Christian Deed.

A couple of stops later, however, the man with the Wonder Bread nudged me. I opened my eyes and saw that he was holding out a bologna sandwich for me.

"Would you like one?" he asked.

I didn't know quite how to answer. I was a little flummoxed and my knee-jerk reaction was (a) it was 6:30 in the morning and a bologna sandwich didn't seem to appetizing at that moment, and (b) I didn't want to take any food from them because I assumed they needed it more than me.

So I gave them a smile and said, "No, thanks."

The man with the Wonder Bread shrugged his shoulders and he and the woman went back to their meal.

A few stops later, I got off the train and went to volunteer. It was a good experience. We helped make breakfast, served and chatted with those guests who came to eat what we produced, and then stayed after to clean up.

That night, though, when I went through my version of the Ignatian *examen* prayer and reflected on the day and where I had seen Christ, my mind went not to the volunteer experience, as good as that was. My mind went to the train and the couple who had offered me a sandwich. I sensed the Spirit putting everything into focus, and I heard a variation of Matthew 25:31-46. Instead of verse 42 that says, "I was hungry and you gave me no food," I heard, "I offered you food and you ignored your hunger." No, I wasn't physically hungry, but I'm always desirous to know and experience Christ's presence and I had missed it. I was ready to make space for Jesus in a particular place at a particular time (the volunteer opportunity) and, indeed, he was there. I failed to truly make space for Jesus on the train, however. The memory of that failure to accept the bounty of the Wonder Bread has never left me and it reminds me of the necessity of hospitality, both to offer and to receive it.

Failures and scars

When I was in kindergarten, I got poked in my palm by a pencil. I can't remember how it happened. Maybe I was goofing around with a friend or maybe I was doing what six-year-olds sometimes do and thought, "I wonder what will happen if I press this pencil into my palm . . ." Whatever the reason, the graphite lodged into my skin and, though it's faint, it remains there more than forty years later.

There was a time when I wondered if there was some way I could get it out of there, but I've come to accept it as a quirky, yet fond scar of sorts from what apparently were the dangerous days of being in Mrs. Anderson's kindergarten class.

There is no doubt that failure leaves scars. Even when writing this book, and I'd have moments of failure in my professional and personal life, I'd respond in unhealthy ways and I'd think, "What is my problem? I'm *writing* about this and I'm still floored when I mess up."

I'm not sure that will ever change. But I hope that you and I, in time, can see that when we "fail different," we grow personally as well as in our ministry. They may leave scars, but also be reminders of times when we hoped and risked (and failed) for Christ's sake.

NOTES

Chapter 1: Taking a Fresh Look at Failure

1. *Born Losers: A History of Failure in America*, Scott Sandage, p. 1
2. http://www.nytimes.com/2009/08/09/magazine/09FOB-on language-t.html?_r=0. Accessed February 20, 2017.
3. http://www.nytimes.com/2009/08/09/magazine/09FOB-on language-t.html?_r=0. Accessed February 20, 2017.
4. Larry Sonner, phone interview, September 2, 2015.
5. http://www.pewforum.org/2015/05/12/americas-changing -religious-landscape/. Accessed February 20, 2017.
6. http://religionnews.com/2015/06/02/mainline-decline-depends -on-what-youre-counting/. Accessed February 20, 2017.
7. From *A Heart Strangely Warmed,* p. 78
8. From *A Heart Strangely Warmed*, p. 254
9. Robert Schnase, phone interview, September 9, 2015,
10. *The Power of Habit: Why We Do What We Do In Life and Business*, Charles Duhigg, p. 104
11. http://www.fastcompany.com/3038446/innovation-agents /failure-has-never-been-more-successful. Accessed February 20, 2017.

Chapter 2: Belovedness Is Our Home Station

1. http://www.patheos.com/blogs/rogereolson/2013/01/did-karl-barth-really-say-jesus-loves-me-this-i-know/. Accessed February 20, 2017.
2. *Life of the Beloved*, Henri Nouwen, p. 53
3. *Life of the Beloved*, p. 72
4. *Abba's Child*, Brendan Manning, p. 33
5. http://www.paulgraham.com/love.html. Accessed February 20, 2017.
6. *Penguin Classics: The Imitation of Christ*, Thomas A Kempis, p. 10,
7. *Abba's Child*, p. 51
8. *Abba's Child*, p. 51
9. *Life of the Beloved*, pp. 43, 45
10. *A Heart Strangely Warmed*, p. 25
11. *A Heart Strangely Warmed*, p. 28
12. *A Heart Strangely Warmed*, p. 36
13. Phoenician Tian Longxiu, personal email, May 21, 2016.

Chapter 3: The Bible Tells Me So

1. *Amazing Grace: A Vocabulary of Faith*, by Kathleen Norris, p. 94
2. *Amazing Grace*, p. 95
3. *Amazing Grace*, p. 95
4. *The Cross and the Lynching Tree*, James Cone, p. 2
5. *New Interpreter's Bible, Vol. IX*, p. 45
6. "Zechariah's Problem," *The Christian Century* 132, no. 25 [December 3, 2015])

7. *Planetwalker*, John Francis, p. 46

8. https://www.ted.com/talks/john_francis_walks_the_earth ?language=en. Accessed February 20, 2017.

Chapter 4: How to Succeed While Failing

1. http://freakonomics.com/podcast/peak/. Accessed February 20, 2017.

2. Beth Ann Estock, personal email, May 26, 2016.

3. *Steve Jobs*, Walter Isaacson, p. 330

4. Zach Kerzee, phone interview, May 4, 2016.

5. "Goals Gone Wild: The Systematic Side Effects of Over-Prescribing Goal Setting," http://hbswk.hbs.edu/item/goals -gone-wild-the-systematic-side-effects-of-over-prescribing-goal -setting, p. 2. Accessed February 20, 2017.

6. "Goals Gone Wild: The Systematic Side Effects of Over-Prescribing Goal Setting," p. 16.

7. http://legacy.ewb.ca/en/whoweare/accountable/failure.html. Accessed February 20, 2017.

8. *Natural Church Development: A Guide to Eight Essential Qualities of Healthy* Churches, Christian A. Schwarz, p. 39

9. *Between Heaven and Mirth: Why Joy, Humor, and Laughter Are at the Heart of the Spiritual Life* by James Martin, SJ, pp. 54-55

10. http://www.benjerry.com/whats-new/flavor-graveyard-depinted. Accessed February 20, 2017.

11. https://www.backstage.com/galleries/12-actors-who-dont-watch -their-own-performances/. Accessed March 9, 2017.

12. *Rising Strong: The Reckoning. The Rumble. The Revolution*, Brené Brown, p. xxv

Chapter 5: Living with the Pain of Failure

1. *European Journal of Pain*, "Does Failure Hurt? The effects of failure feedback on pain report, pain tolerance and pain avoidance," December 2000, Vol. 4, Issue 4, pp. 335-346

2. *Rising Strong*, Brené Brown, p. xxv

3. http://www.forbes.com/sites/billfischer/2016/03/07/we-are -failing-at-failing/. Accessed February 20, 2017.

4. *Envy*, Joseph Epstein, p. 19

5. George Linney, phone interview, February 2, 2016.

6. *Heart Strangely Warmed*, Jonathan Dean, p. 5

7. *Heart Strangely Warmed*, Jonathan Dean, p. 28

8. *Heart Strangely Warmed,* Jonathan Dean, p. 29

9. *Sabbatical Journey*, Henri Nouwen, p. 5

10. *Sabbatical Journey*, Henri Nouwen, p. 5

11. *Sabbatical Journey*, Nouwen, p. 6

12. *Giraffes Can't Dance*, Guy Parker-Reese

Chapter 6: The Gifts That Failure Provides

1. http://www.nytimes.com/1994/01/28/arts/art-in-review-011215. html. Accessed February 20, 2017.

2. Used by permission of Mary Proctor.

3. This quote and others about this story came from an online article in the Washington Post, April 28, 2016, "Why it feels so good to read about this Princeton professor's failures" by Ann Swanson. https://www.washingtonpost.com/news/wonk /wp/2016/04/28/it-feels-really-good-to-read-about-this-princeton -professors-failures/. Accessed February 20, 2017.

4. I got this insight from the *New Interpreter's Bible*, Vol. X, p. 711

5. https://www.churchleadership.com/leading-ideas/cool-church -isnt-what-it-used-to-be/. Accessed February 20, 2017.

6. "The True Eccentric," p. 3, *Christian Century*, June 8, 2016

7. *Why Christian?*, Douglas John Hall, p. 103

8. Paul Laurence Dunbar, "Sympathy," public domain, found at https://www.poetryfoundation.org/poems-and-poets/poems /detail/46459. Accessed February 20, 2017.

9. *The Strength of Gideon: And Other Stories*, Paul Dunbar, p. 307

10. *Dictionary of Westminster Theological Terms*, Donald K. McKim, p. 89

11. http://www.theodore-roosevelt.com/images/research/speeches /maninthearena.pdf. Accessed February 20, 2017.

12. *Dancing Standing Still: Healing the World from a Place of Prayer,* Richard Rohr pp. 100, 103.

13. Jud Curry, personal correspondence, June 2, 2016.

14. *Making Room: Recovering Hospitality as a Christian Tradition*, by Christine Pohl, p. 31

15. *Making Room: Recovering Hospitality as a Christian Tradition*, by Christine Pohl, p. 39

CPSIA information can be obtained
at www.ICGtesting.com
Printed in the USA
BVHW042352060321
601778BV00018B/113

9 780881 778786